Religion and Magic

Religion and Magic

.

Approaches and Theories

.

Graham Cunningham

Edinburgh University Press

©Graham Cunningham, 1999

Edinburgh University Press
22 George Square, Edinburgh

Typeset in New Baskerville
by Tradespools Ltd, Frome, and
printed and bound in Great Britain by
MPG Books, Bodmin

A CIP record for this book is available from the British Library

ISBN 0 7186 1013 8

Contents

.

Introduction

.

O VER THE PAST 100 years the study of religion and magic, or of the sacred (to use a term sometimes employed to refer to both), has changed dramatically. It has expanded outside the traditional confines of theology and philosophy to become part of modern disciplines such as anthropology, sociology and psychology, while theology has been joined by newly founded disciplines such as religious studies, comparative religions and the history of religions. Concentrating on these new disciplines, this book provides a brief survey of some of the most important developments in the study of the sacred during this period of change.

While religious studies and its fellow disciplines belong to the humanities, three of the other disciplines covered – anthropology, sociology and psychology – belong to the social sciences, the group of overlapping fields of study concerned with human behaviour, society and the interaction between individuals and groups within society. Two of these social sciences can be described fairly straightforwardly. Psychology, broadly speaking, is the study of mental processes and of their effect on human behaviour, while sociology is the study of societies mainly brought into being by the industrial transformations of the past two or three centuries.

Distinguishing between sociology and anthropology is more difficult, partly because of the extent to which their concerns overlap and partly because of a problem with terminology. Literally anthropology means the study of man, being derived from the Greek word *anthropos* meaning man in the sense of human rather than male. In practice, however, anthropology tends to be primarily concerned with people in societies outside the remit of sociology, raising the problem of how to describe such societies. Most descriptions, such as primitive and exotic, have negative implications, while others, such as pre-industrial, suggest that they precede a different type of society. The term used in this book is oral, indicating that they are societies that do not have the technology of writing, as distinct from literate societies which do. The term is again not ideal – it indicates a lack rather than what is better regarded as a difference and suggests that differences between societies relate solely to the possession of a particular technology – but it seems more neutral than the various other descriptions which have been proposed.

In addition to covering the study of the sacred in a wide range of disciplines, the book spans a broad period, concentrating on developments between approximately 1870 and 1970. To present this survey in manageable terms, it is arranged chronologically in terms of different types of approach, with some of these approaches respecting national and disciplinary boundaries and some crossing them. Providing an exact definition of what is meant by approach in this context is difficult. In one sense the approaches are different interpretations of magical and religious beliefs and practices. More broadly, however, the approaches include three elements, to varying degrees in each type of approach: assumptions about what people are like and what motivates their behaviour and beliefs, theories explaining such behaviour and beliefs, and preferences in terms of research method used. While the book concentrates on approaches specifically to religion and magic, the approaches of certain scholars to the broader subject-matters of their disciplines are also discussed.

In many ways the period covered by the book can be regarded as modern, although opinions differ on when the modern age began. One standard dictionary definition of modern is that it refers to the period in European history from the end of the Middle Ages onwards, that is from the fifteenth century onwards. Other definitions are more narrow. For example, the founder of modern philosophy is often held to be Descartes (1596–1650), famous for arguing that the existence of a thought proves the existence of a thinker, or as he put it 'I think therefore I am'. In the more specific terms of the philosophy of religion, however, the work of Hegel (1770–1831) can be regarded as representing a more significant turning point and it is with a discussion of Hegel that this book begins.

Before Hegel, studies of religion had tended to be theological, that is primarily concerned with studying the nature of the divine, or more specifically in Christian terms with the study of God. Hegel, however, placed as much emphasis on religious believers as on what he referred to as the object of their beliefs. In doing so he offered a less negative interpretation of non-Christian religions, and of magic, than had previously been the case. Moreover, his inclusion of the study of believers within the study of religion can be viewed as prefiguring the way the sacred has been studied in modern disciplines. In addition to Hegel's studies of the sacred, Chapter 1 discusses the work of two other German scholars, Marx, the principal nineteenth-century founder of communism, and Weber, one of the founders of sociology as an academic discipline at the beginning of the twentieth century.

These three German scholars were interested in identifying the origins of religion, as were the three British scholars from the second half of the nineteenth century who are discussed in Chapter 2. These British scholars – Spencer, Tylor and Frazer – took an intellectualist approach to religion, interpreting it as a means of explaining events by attributing them to divine intervention. Tylor's role in establishing anthropology as an academic discipline was as important as Weber's in sociology and in 1886 he was appointed Europe's first professor of anthropology.

Chapter 3 concentrates on the work of three scholars from the first half of the twentieth century who took an emotionalist approach to the sacred, interpreting magic and religion as the release of different types of emotion. Two of these scholars, Marett and Malinowski, were anthropologists who taught primarily in Britain, while the third is the Austrian psychologist Freud, whose investigation of the unconscious transformed the study of the human mind. Malinowski also transformed his discipline, turning anthropology from the armchair study of similarities between different societies to an approach emphasising fieldwork and the individual qualities of specific societies.

Chapter 4 traces developments in the twentieth century in what is referred to as the phenomenological study of religion. This type of approach owes its origins to a school of philosophy which emphasises the study of phenomena, that is objects as we experience or perceive them as distinct from the objects themselves. In relation to the study of the sacred, phenomenological approaches have been particularly favoured by historians of religion and concentrate on describing what religious believers feel and experience. Such approaches are represented in this chapter by the work of three scholars: Otto, whose studies of the sacred span the divide between theology and the history of religions; Eliade, arguably the twentieth century's foremost historian of religions; and Smart, who founded Britain's first major religious studies department and is now a professor of comparative religions in the United States. Also discussed in this chapter is the work of the Swiss psychologist Jung, a one-time collaborator with Freud who went on to found his own school of psychology and develop ideas about religion that in many ways are similar to those of Otto and Eliade.

Chapter 5 returns to the disciplines of sociology and anthropology. Weber has already been mentioned as one of the founding fathers of sociology. The other major figure responsible for establishing the discipline was the French scholar Durkheim, who in 1913 became Europe's first professor of sociology. Among the many contributions of Durkheim, and of his colleagues such as Mauss, to the study of religion was an argument, now referred to broadly as structural-functional, that religion functions to maintain a society and reflects its social structure. While much of the work of Durkheim and his colleagues was brought to an end by the First World War, it exerted a strong influence on British scholars, including Radcliffe-Brown who in the late 1930s replaced Malinowski as the leading British anthropologist and whose work is also discussed in this chapter.

The remaining five chapters concentrate on developments in the study of the sacred since the end of the Second World War. Chapter 6 focuses on approaches to religion that interpret it as various types of symbolic system. One of these approaches, referred to as symbolist and represented here by the British anthropologists Douglas and Beattie, continues Durkheim's work and argues that religion symbolises social structure and social values. However, anthropological interpretation of the symbolic nature of religion has been influenced by scholars other than Durkheim, in particular by two of his Continental contemporaries, Lévy-Bruhl and van Gennep, whose work this chapter begins by discussing. Three further post-war symbolic approaches to the sacred are discussed in this chapter. One, by Turner, argues that certain items used in ritual symbolise basic human biological and psychological processes. Another, by Tambiah, relates magical symbolism to figurative uses of language such as metaphor. The third, the distinctive contribution of the American anthropologist Geertz, interprets religion as providing symbols of cosmic order.

Despite the Continental influence on British anthropology, the intellectualist tradition has never entirely disappeared because part of its definition of religion, that it requires a belief in spiritual beings, has remained the one in most popular use. However, from approximately the 1960s onwards, other aspects of the intellectualist tradition were revived which are discussed in Chapter 7. This intellectualist revival, interpreting religion again as a means of explaining events but emphasising that it is also a means of influencing events by appealing for divine intervention, is represented here by the work of Goody, Jarvie, Horton and Skorupski.

In his own country Durkheim's influence was somewhat different, as is discussed in Chapter 8. The dominant figure in French anthropology from approximately the 1950s onwards was Lévi-Strauss, who was one of the leading contributors to a school of thought referred to as structuralism. While Durkheim argued that a society's religion reflects and thus symbolises its social structure, Lévi-Strauss argued that both reflect the unconscious structuring activity of the mind, and that both are symbolic structures which can be interpreted in the same way as the primary symbolic structure, language. Lévi-Strauss's structural approach has influenced other anthropologists, for example the two other scholars discussed in this chapter: the British anthropologist Leach and the French anthropologist Godelier, whose work combines structuralism with Marxism and thus provides an example of Marx's continuing influence in the twentieth century.

The emphasis in Lévi-Strauss's work on the unconscious structuring activity of the mind returns us to the discipline of psychology. It also points forward to a recent trend in anthropology, discussed in Chapter 9: cognitive approaches that relate religion to different types of mental processes or cognitive mechanisms. Various examples of such approaches are discussed, reflecting the breadth of cognitive science as a discipline encompassing psychology, linguistics – that is the study of language – and artificial intelligence – that is the attempt to create computers which think like humans and which in doing so may shed light on our mental processes. One example of a cognitive approach to religion, by Sperber, returns to the subject of symbolism, relating it to a specific cognitive mechanism. Another, by Lawson and McCauley, turns to linguistics rather than psychology, interpreting religion in the light of theories about the relationship between a language's deep structure and the speech generated by that structure. Another, by Boyer, moves discussion of religion into the area of artificial intelligence and the possibility of clarifying the processes that constitute human cognition.

The final type of approach discussed is feminism, represented in Chapter 10 by the work of the French post-structuralist Kristeva and the American theologian and philosopher Daly. However, in many ways to discuss feminism as one among many approaches to religion is inadequate because one of its central arguments, that much scholarship written by men does insufficient justice to the experience of half of the world's population, and that religion itself has contributed to this bias, poses a fundamental challenge to other approaches.

The book ends by assessing what many of the scholars discussed in previous chapters have predicted for religion, namely its demise or decline – a process referred to as secularisation – or a change in its nature, from a concern with material ends such as good health to a concern with more spiritual matters. The concluding chapter discusses the accuracy of these predictions, pointing to evidence that contradicts them and indicates not only the survival and continuing influence of established religions but also the formation of new religious configurations.

While developments in the study of the sacred in modern disciplines can be surveyed from the perspective of these types of approach, they can be viewed in other ways, for example in terms of disagreements about the relationship between the humanities disciplines, the social sciences and the natural sciences such as physics and biology. These disagreements are discussed in the text but a brief overview can be presented here. Some social scientists argue that the theoretical frameworks and experimental methods of the natural sciences can be applied in the social sciences. For example, the British intellectualist Spencer (Chapter 2) applied the principles of species evolution developed in biology to the evolution of societies. Other social scientists regard such applications as inappropriate, arguing that there is an essential difference between the subject-matters of the natural and social sciences in that the social sciences involve the study of human behaviour as distinct from the study of the physical world. Members of this opposite camp, such as the German sociologist Weber (Chapter 1), tend to study the social sciences in ways influenced by traditional approaches within the humanities.

A third camp or school of thought, represented in this book in particular by the discipline of cognitive science (Chapter 9), takes an intermediate position, recognising a distinction between the subject-matters of the natural and social sciences but arguing that this requires the development of new theories and research procedures rather than the adoption of humanities-influenced approaches. A fourth camp also exists, represented by structuralism (Chapter 8), which pursues a radical change to both the social sciences and the humanities that would bring the two into alignment. In addition, some humanities scholars, such as the feminist historian of religions Kraemer (Chapter 10), argue that some of the more traditional approaches in the social sciences are appropriate to the humanities.

Another perspective from which to view the study of the sacred in modern disciplines is in relation to three sets of opposites: symbolic versus practical, society versus individual and consensus versus conflict. The relationship between these sets of opposites and the different types of approach is again discussed in more detail in the text but some examples can be given here.

The first set of opposites, symbolic versus practical, relates primarily to the twentieth-century dispute between symbolic approaches which interpret religion as a symbolic system of various kinds (Chapter 6) and intellectualist approaches which interpret religion not only as a way of explaining events by attributing them to divine intervention but also as a means of influencing events by appealing for such intervention, that is as a means of achieving practical results (Chapter 7). Various terms have been used to express this opposition: symbolic, mystical, expressive and ritual on the one hand, and practical, instrumental, technical, empirical and scientific on the other. While most of the scholars who regard religion as symbolic or its equivalent include magic within that category, some exclude it. For example, one anthropologist, Malinowski (Chapter 3), distinguished between magic as practical and religion as expressive, that is as releasing emotions aroused by events such as birth and death. Weber proposed a somewhat similar distinction between magical, this-worldly aims, such as prosperity, and religious, other-worldly concerns which bring meaning rather than material success to social life (Chapter 1).

An example of the opposition between the individual and society is provided by the intellectualists (Chapter 7) and a particular type of symbolic approach to religion, the symbolists, who argue that religion symbolises social structure and social values (Chapter 6). This symbolist emphasis on the importance of society contrasts with the intellectualist conception of individuals seeking explanations for events and turning for assistance to deities.

The opposition between the individual and society relates to the third set of opposites, that between conflict and consensus. It has often been argued that symbolist approaches that interpret religion as symbolising social structure, and thus as complementing social structure in such a way as to maintain it, present a consensus view of a society, one in which all of its members are broadly in agreement and which therefore ignores the question of conflict within a society. This in turn raises the broader question of how change is to be explained, given that it is often described in terms of conflict. In the opposition between consensus and conflict, as in the opposition between society and the individual, Durkheim's work (Chapter 5) can be viewed as representing one school of sociological thought tending towards the former and Weber's (Chapter 1) as a second school tending towards the latter.

Having established broadly what the book covers, it is worth noting some of its limitations and discussing its method in more detail. An immediately apparent limitation is that the book surveys developments in the study of the sacred in modern disciplines, thus generally excluding theology and the philosophy of religion. This limitation, however, has the advantage of focusing on approaches to religion that have a certain unity in terms of both their concerns and their development. For similar reasons more recent interpretations of religion have also been omitted. A further limitation is that the book concentrates on studies of the sacred written by Western, particularly European, scholars. Again this limitation can be defended on the grounds of the unity it allows. However, it should be acknowledged that the lack of reference to studies of the sacred written by scholars outside Western culture indicates no disrespect but rather the author's own ignorance.

Within the disciplines and period covered, the question arises of what should be selected for inclusion. Any survey is inevitably selective, particularly one as brief as this, and it should be emphasised that this book is merely one of many possible surveys. However, there is a consensus of opinion about which approaches to religion, and which scholars and which of their publications, are significant, and it is this consensus that the book aims to reflect.

Questions also arise in relation to chronology and the types of approach into which the scholars have been categorised. The book broadly presents a historical survey based on types of approach, and within that of the scholars who have adopted such an approach and then of their particular publications. This presents some problems in relation to the approaches: sharp lines cannot always be drawn between different types of approach and not all the scholars discussed fit neatly into one particular type. In such cases the demarcation problems are discussed in the text. In addition, the chronological ride is occasionally somewhat bumpy because the approaches, and the scholars who have adopted them, do not always form a straightforward historical sequence. To provide assistance on this ride, the dates of scholars whose careers preceded the Second World War are given in the text.

The aim throughout has been to describe the types of approach, and summarise the work of the various scholars, as clearly and simply as is possible. In addition, the book aims to be accurate, a tall order given the difficulties inherent in summarising often complex ideas. To compensate for any inaccuracy in the summaries, the book relies as much as possible on quotations from the original writings, with any italics being those of the authors. The dates these writings were originally published are specified in the text, while the references are to the most recent, or most readily available, editions in English. Full details of these editions are given in the bibliography, which also cites three further publications on this subject to each of which this book is indebted.

The summaries of particular scholars' work presented in this book are expanded by comparisons with the work of other scholars. Obviously such comparisons, and more indirectly the processes of selection, categorising, summarising and placing in sequence, represent a form of criticism. Beyond that, however, assessment has been kept to a minimum. The book thus provides an introduction to some of the ways in which the sacred has been studied, and an orientation in relation to some of the issues involved in such a study, with a view to encouraging further reading within and beyond the works that have been introduced.

1

·

German pioneers

·

THIS CHAPTER DISCUSSES THE work of three German scholars –
Hegel, Marx and Weber – each of whom can be regarded as
a pioneer: Hegel for his fundamental contributions to philosophy;
Marx for his influence on the set of socio-economic theories and
practices which now bears his name, Marxism; and Weber for his
role in establishing sociology as an academic discipline. While these
scholars worked within different disciplines, to a degree their concerns overlapped. In relation to religion each sought to identify its
origins, and, more broadly, each had an interest in the question of
the relationship between the mental realm of ideas and the material
world in which we live. Hegel placed particular emphasis on the
former and Marx on the latter, while Weber steered a middle path
between the two.

Despite this difference in perspective, both Hegel and Marx envisaged history as a process of dialectical progress, a process (discussed
further below) which involves movement from a period of thesis to an
opposite period of antithesis and then on to a period of synthesis. In
contrast, Weber regarded people less as participants in such broad
processes and more as agents influencing their own destinies. However, similarities also exist between Marx and Weber in that both
influenced a twentieth-century school of sociological thought referred
to as conflict theory. This school of thought accuses the type of
structural-functional approach discussed in Chapter 5 of ignoring the
divisive nature of social conflict and presenting a consensus view of
society. Advocates of conflict theory divide broadly into two camps,
Marxist and pluralist, influenced by Marx and Weber respectively and
reflecting each scholar's particular orientation, with the former

emphasising class conflict and the latter rival interest groups formed as much by their values and beliefs as by their socio-economic positions.

One particular aspect of Hegel's work also relates to other approaches to the sacred discussed later in this book. A central concern of the nineteenth century was evolution, both of species and of societies: Darwin's *The Origin of the Species* was published in 1859 while other scholars in the second half of the century, in particular Spencer whose work is discussed in the next chapter, described the evolution of societies in similar terms. Hegel's own discussion of religion, which places religions from various times and places into a temporal sequence, represents an early indication of the century's interest in social or cultural evolution.

Hegel

G. W. F. Hegel (1770–1831) is among the most influential, and most difficult, of modern philosophers. The relative ordinariness of his academic life was in contrast to the events that took place during it: in 1789 the Bastille, a fortress in Paris then serving as a prison, was destroyed at the beginning of the French Revolution, a revolution that Hegel welcomed and that led to the redrawing of the political map of western Europe. The best known event in the French Revolution is probably the guillotining of the French king, an event that represents only one, republican aspect of the revolution which also involved a series of liberalising reforms, including the introduction of more popular and more democratic laws.

Disputes that broke out between the various factions involved in the Revolution led eventually to the rise to power of Napoleon who became Emperor of France in 1804. He continued the programme of political, legal and administrative reforms begun by the revolution as well as establishing an extensive European empire. At the time of the Revolution what is now called Germany consisted of numerous principalities forming part of the Holy Roman Empire, ruled by an emperor based in Austria. Napoleon's military victories over the Austrian Emperor's forces brought about the end of this thousand-year-old empire and instituted a period of French domination and of liberal reform in the lands over which Napoleon ruled. The defeat of Napoleon, first at Leipzig in 1813 and finally at Waterloo two years later, put an end to both.

Against this backdrop of Continental wars, in which England and the Russian Empire also opposed Napoleon, Hegel's academic career developed slowly. He studied philosophy and theology at a seminary at Tübingen before working as a private tutor until 1799. In that year he moved to Jena to lecture privately to the town's university students, while working on his own publications. The deadline for delivering the manuscript of his first major work, *The Phenomenology of Spirit*, coincided with the arrival of triumphant French troops in 1806. The French occupation led to the closure of Jena's university and Hegel moved elsewhere to work as headmaster of a secondary school. However, in 1816, now in his forties, he returned to university life, becoming professor of philosophy at Heidelberg University and moving two years later to the chair of philosophy at Berlin University, where he lectured until his death in 1831.

In *The Phenomenology of Spirit* Hegel develops his concept of *Geist*, a German word that can be understood in two ways, corresponding to two of the meanings of the English word 'spirit' used here in translating the book's title. In one sense the word refers to a person's spirit: their intangible being in contrast to their physical presence, a distinction often expressed in terms of mind versus matter. In another sense the word refers to a supernatural being, as in the phrase *der Heilige Geist* (the Holy Ghost or Spirit), in which sense it sometimes seems to be used by Hegel as a synonym for God. More generally, however, Hegel's use of the term can be viewed as including both senses: *Geist* is a kind of impersonal absolute or unity which he regards as including both human minds and the objects those minds perceive.

The relationship between mind and its perception of objects relates to the second noun in the title of this book. In general terms phenomenology is the study of phenomena, that is things as they appear to us or are experienced by us as distinct from things as they are; an often cited example of this distinction being the difference between the moon we see as a small crescent or ball and its actual size. However, the book's title indicates that Hegel's specific concern is Spirit as it appears to itself, and the book charts what Hegel regards as Spirit's progress through time to a full and unified awareness of itself and all that it embraces.

Geist is also a central concept in Hegel's most comprehensive work on religion, *Lectures on the Philosophy of Religion*. As the title of this book suggests, it is based on lectures given by Hegel, in this instance ones that he gave in Berlin. The first edition was published in 1832, the year after Hegel's death, compiled from his lecture outlines and from records made by students of lectures delivered at different sessions. A revised edition was published in 1840 following the identification of more of Hegel's own notes and outlines.

In this book Hegel defines religion as 'consciousness of God in general'[1] and identifies magic as the earliest type of religion, taking 'the form of power over nature'.[2] He argues that understanding religion requires a synthesis of two elements, 'the *object* [the divine] that is *in* religion, and consciousness, i.e. the *subject*, the human being that comports itself toward that object'.[3] While the study of religion had previously emphasised the divine, Hegel regards the human role as equally important: 'The subjective and cultic aspect of religion is, therefore, the other essential element in the consideration of religion generally.'[4] In addition, Hegel considers that a proper understanding of religion requires the study of all its types or manifestations, not simply those deemed theologically valid. As he puts it, no matter 'what supremely marvellous and bizarre flights of fancy the nations have hit upon in their representations of the divine ... it is *human beings* who have lighted upon such religions, so there must be *reason* in them'.[5] And it is this reason that the study of religion should aim to recover.

The book also provides an example of Hegel's use of dialectic. In logic or reasoning dialectic refers to the practice of identifying the truth of an opinion through discussion, or more specifically of identifying the arguments both for a thesis and against it, its antithesis, in such a way that the contradictions between the thesis and antithesis are resolved at a higher level of truth that synthesises the two. Hegel expanded the term to refer not merely to a process of reasoning but to a process in history, consisting of a development from a period of thesis found to contain inconsistencies to a period characterised as its opposite or antithesis. This period is similarly found to be wanting and is replaced by a period of synthesis that combines the merits of the preceding thesis and antithesis. Should that synthesis also turn out to be inadequate, it then becomes a thesis for a further dialectical movement.

In *Lectures on the Philosophy of Religion* Hegel argues that the development of religion has been from a thesis of immanent religion in which the divine was viewed as being present in this world, to an antithesis of transcendent religion in which the divine was viewed as being outside this world, and finally to a successful synthesis of the two in which the divine is viewed as being both immanent and transcendent. While this example indicates the sometimes broad sweep of Hegelian dialectic, on other levels it can be viewed less grandly as a way of representing human experience as a constantly interactive process.

Looking in more detail at the three stages in Hegel's sequence, and continuing to translate *Geist* as Spirit, the first is the religion of nature,

4

an essentially immanent stage in which Spirit is part of nature. This stage consists primarily of both past and present Eastern religions, with ancient Egyptian religion representing its peak and being preceded by Zoroastrianism, Hinduism and Buddhism. At its beginning is magic, 'the oldest, rawest, crudest form of religion',[6] characterised by the manipulation of nature. Hegel's evidence for this form of religion comes from African tribes and Eskimos (Innuits): 'The religion of magic is still found today among wholly crude and barbarous peoples such as the Eskimos.'[7] The second stage in Hegel's sequence comprises the Greek, Roman and Jewish religions and is essentially transcendent: Spirit is elevated above nature.

The third stage represents a synthesis of the previous two, being a whole which is both immanent and transcendent, and is represented only by Christianity, 'the consummate religion'.[8] The privileged position that Hegel gives Christianity would now be disputed by many for favouring Western values and traditions. However, Hegel's view of God is far from traditional because his argument appears to be that Spirit – God in relation to the final stage of Christianity – can only fully realise itself when nature is perceived to be the expression of Spirit, and thus that Spirit can only fully realise itself in relation to the material world in which we live and our perception of that world.

Marx

Karl Marx (1818–83), a social scientist and revolutionary, studied philosophy at Berlin University not long after Hegel's death when the latter's influence was still strong. However, other influences were also in play at German universities at this time. The liberalism associated with the French Revolution and furthered by the Napoleonic conquests had been defeated, and the restored hereditary rulers were determined to maintain their recovered positions by promoting traditional authority and religion. Within the universities little dissent was allowed to this tradition, leaving no academic place for an avowed atheist and political radical such as Marx.

Marx turned instead to journalism, becoming editor of a liberal newspaper in Cologne in 1842. However, the newspaper, too, succumbed to conservative pressure and was closed by censors the next year. Marx left Germany, first for Paris and then in 1845 for Brussels, devoting his time and energies to studying economics and promoting the cause of communism. While communism supports some liberal reforms it aims at a more thorough restructuring of society, involving the overthrow by the working classes of the classes regarded as their economic and political oppressors, and the creation of a classless society whose members give according to their abilities and receive according to their needs. It was in Paris that Marx formed his lifelong partnership with Friedrich Engels (1820–95), with whom he wrote *The Communist Manifesto*.

After the outbreak of a series of small-scale republican revolutions in 1848 Marx returned to newspaper-editing in Cologne. However, the newspaper was closed by the conservative counter-reaction in the next year and Marx and Engels emigrated to England, Marx to London and Engels to Manchester. In London Marx continued his research, writing and political activity until his death in 1883. His work preceded the establishing of sociology as an academic discipline and covered a wide range of subjects, including economics, politics, history and philosophy as well as what is now termed sociology. In this work he was supported financially by Engels whose family had business interests in Manchester. Engels also acted as a populariser and interpreter of Marx's work, creating the problem of untangling Marx's own voice from the interpretive tradition begun by Engels and developed by subsequent Marxists.

Marx's own most famous statement on religion, made in an article published in 1844, is that 'religion is the *opium* of the people'.[9] In the same article Marx emphasises his position as an atheist, simultaneously stressing the primacy of social rather than individual forces by arguing that religion is solely a social construction. For example, he comments: '*Man makes religion*, religion does not make man ... But *man* is no abstract being squatting outside the world. Man is *the world of man*, the state, society. This state, this society, produce religion.'[10]

Elsewhere Marx examines the role that religion performs in society, distinguishing between a society's economic base and its superstructure to which religion belongs. For Marx a society's economic base includes both what he refers to as the forces or means of production – the natural resources, labour and technology available to a society – and the relations of production – the way those forces are organised, including the relations between a society's members, more often referred to as social structure. Resting on this economic base is a society's superstructure, that is its legal, political and religious institutions and its ideologies. In general use ideology is a neutral term referring to a socially significant set of beliefs and ideas. Marx, however, used the term in a more complex and more negative sense. For Marx an ideology is not only a belief that is false but also one that falsifies, that is prevents the working classes from realising their oppression and enables ruling classes to endorse their ascendancy as being part of the natural order of things. Thus, for example, Marx attributed Christianity's institutional status to its preaching of an ethics of submission that benefits ruling classes, allowing them to exploit the working classes while at the same time obscuring that exploitation.

Marx's emphasis on the role of the economic base is often presented as contrasting with Hegel's emphasis on the mental realm of *Geist*. The philosophies of both Hegel and Marx are not straightforward in relation to this question. Marx envisaged a complex relationship between the two aspects of the economic base, referred to as the mode of production, and between the economic base and the superstructure, and Hegel a similarly complex relationship between nature and *Geist*. Broadly speaking Marx regarded a society's economic base as ultimately shaping or determining its superstructure while Hegel placed more emphasis on *Geist*. A similar contrast emerges in both scholars' large-scale historical studies, with Hegel envisaging development as a kind of dialectical march towards *Geist*'s self-knowledge, which culminates in Christianity, and Marx envisaging it as a series of class conflicts culminating in communism when religion would no longer be needed and would therefore disappear.

However, despite these differences in perspectives, both scholars regarded the relationships they discussed as essentially interactive. Marx therefore viewed the economic base as both determining and being determined by the superstructure, which aligns him with Hegel's dialectical approach. This suggests that, while both scholars had different emphases, neither adopted an unqualified determinism, neither Marx reducing historical development to socio-economic causes alone nor Hegel to mental or spiritual causes alone.

More straightforwardly Marx followed Hegel in regarding the earliest religion as having been one of nature. This origin of religion is proposed in *The German Ideology*, written jointly with Engels in the 1840s but not published until later, which also briefly specifies the interactive nature of the relationship between a society's economic base and its religion: 'This natural religion or this particular relation of man to nature is determined by the form of society and vice versa.'[11] Engels comments similarly in a letter written in 1890:

> These various false conceptions of nature, of man's own being, of spirits, magic forces, etc., have for the most part only a negative economic element as their basis; the low economic development of the prehistoric per-

iod is supplemented and also partially conditioned and even caused by the false conceptions of nature.[12]

While Marx took Hegel's historical interests to heart he wrote no description of the development of religion as detailed as Hegel's. Instead he concentrated on socio-economic development, envisaged as moving dialectically from a kind of primitive communism through various stages and types of social exploitation to a fully realised form of communism. Engels, however, offers a brief outline of the development of religion in a work published in 1878. Here he takes a less interactive approach, arguing instead that religious change is caused by socio-economic change, but continuing to emphasise religion's ideological role of endorsing or legitimating exploitation. As he puts it: 'All religion is nothing but the fantastic reflection in men's minds of those external forces which control their daily life, a reflection in which the terrestrial forces assume the form of supernatural forces.'[13]

As before, Engels suggests that the first terrestrial forces to have been given such supernatural status were the forces of nature. As societies had become more structured, it was their controlling social forces that had been accorded this status: 'Social forces begin to be active – forces which confront man as equally alien and at first equally inexplicable, dominating him with the same apparent natural necessity as the forces of nature themselves.'[14] Monotheism occurred at a further stage in economic development: 'All the natural and social attributes of the numerous gods are transferred to *one* almighty god, who is but a reflection of the abstract man. Such was the origin of monotheism.'[15] In this stage religion continues 'to exist as the ... form of men's relation to the alien natural and social forces which dominate them',[16] that is 'men are dominated by the economic conditions created by themselves ... as if by an alien force'.[17]

However, in an article written in 1886, Engels offers a different account of the origin of religion, placing less emphasis on the economic base and more, like the nineteenth-century intellectualists discussed in the next chapter, on people's attempts to explain aspects of the world around them. For example, he argues that the concept of the soul arose from speculation about dreams: 'Men ... under the stimulus of dream apparitions came to believe that their thinking and sensation were not activities of their bodies, but of a distinct soul which inhabits the body and leaves it at death.'[18] Similarly the concept of the soul's immortality derived from conjecture: 'Not religious desire for consolation, but the quandary arising from the common universal ignorance of what to do with this soul ... after the death of the body led in a general way to the tedious notion of personal immortality.'[19] The origin of the first deities is also attributed to such speculation: 'In an exactly similar manner the first gods arose through the personification of natural forces.'[20]

Weber
·

The establishment of sociology as a distinctive academic discipline can be traced through the life of the third German scholar discussed in this chapter, Max Weber (1864–1920). When he studied at university and when he was given his first academic appointments, sociology as such was not an academic option, and it was only late in his life that he received his first post in that discipline. Weber studied philosophy, economics, history and law at various German universities before embarking on an academic career, working in the economics faculty at Freiburg University from 1894 and moving to the same faculty at Heidelberg University in 1897. A long period of illness followed, during which Weber continued to research and write until the onset of the First World War in 1914. Throughout the war he worked as a hospital administrator.

During the course of this war (fought between the Allies – initially Britain, France and the Russian Empire – and the Central Powers – most of the countries from Germany to Turkey) the Russian Revolution began, leading to the creation of a Soviet republic based on the principles of Bolshevik communism, a type of communism which stresses the role of a kind of central vanguard group in leading the working classes. At the end of the war in 1918, Weber returned to academic employment, first to the newly created chair of sociology at Vienna University, and then in 1919 to a similar post in Munich, where he died one year later.

Weber's analyses of the relationship between religion and socioeconomics can be viewed as steering a path between Hegel's emphasis on the mental realm and Marx's on the economic base. For example, in *The Protestant Ethic and the Spirit of Capitalism*, published in 1904–5, Weber argues that religious ideas, specifically the Protestant belief that worldly success is a sign of divine favour, contributed to the creation of the capitalist economic system. However, he specifies that such ideas were not the only contributing factors, rather they were ones that had previously been neglected in favour of economic explanations and that formed part of a complex network of causes.

As this example indicates, Weber favoured an approach to the social sciences referred to as hermeneutical or interpretive, arguing that understanding why people act in certain ways involves interpreting what those actions mean to the people performing them. The term hermeneutics was first used in Christian theology where it referred to the interpretation of the Bible. However, in the late nineteenth century the term was taken from theology and used to refer to a method of interpreting not only other types of literature but also those aspects of human behaviour that constitute the social sciences. In particular it was argued that human behaviour should be understood as the actions of free and rational people whose motives can be understood through a process of empathy based partly on shared rationality and partly on an attempt to conceptualise the world in the terms of the performers of the actions. Understanding literature was similarly argued to require regarding the text as an expression of rational activity and attempting to empathise with the author's view of the world.

The emphasis in hermeneutics on people as purposeful agents opposes the theories of Hegel and Marx, which regard individuals as subject to large-scale, law-like processes of dialectical change, leading in Hegel's case to a truer knowledge of reality and in Marx's case to a more egalitarian society. Hermeneutical approaches also oppose the position taken by the other important figure in the early history of sociology as an academic discipline, Durkheim, Weber's French contemporary whose work is discussed in Chapter 5. While Weber favoured a humanities-influenced, interpretive approach to the social sciences, Durkheim argued that the patterns of social life have a similar reality to the physical objects studied in the natural sciences, and that these social or collective facts should be studied not through processes such as empathy but in the same way as natural scientists study the physical world. As a result Durkheim, too, placed much less emphasis on the individual than Weber, arguing that most collective facts precede individuals and that, even when individuals collaborate to create collective facts, a gap exists between their intentions and what they create.

Weber's emphasis on the individual presented him with the problem of generalising from the abundance of human experience. One of his solutions was the use of what is referred to as ideal-type analysis, that is identifying the essential characteristics of an aspect of society in order to construct its ideal or generalised type. Weber applied this form of analysis not only to specific periods and places, for example in his discussion of the rise of capitalism in western Europe, but also on a broader scale, writing monumental studies that examine the development of social institutions and compare different civilisations.

One such study is *Economy and Society*, published in 1921–2 after Weber's death, which includes a section on religious groups in which he examines the origin and subsequent development of religion. Weber begins this analysis by arguing that religion is difficult to define and promising to provide a definition once the various forms of religion have been discussed. However, the question of defining religion is not returned to, and in his discussion Weber identifies similar problems in distinguishing precisely between magic and religion. Like Hegel, he describes the earliest type of religion as having been essentially magical. However, unlike Hegel, he argues that later religions, including Christianity, have retained magical elements, with the exception of one type of Protestantism: 'Only ascetic Protestantism completely eliminated magic.'[21] Weber distinguishes three different types of early, essentially magical religion, between which 'there are many transitions and combinations'.[22] The first type is naturalism in which objects or magicians are thought to be endowed with a power that Weber refers to as charisma; the second type is animism in which spiritual forces are thought to be the source of this charisma; and the third type is symbolism in which charismatic objects symbolise the spiritual forces. The importance of symbolism as creating another level of reality is stressed by Weber:

> Since it is assumed that behind real things and events there is something else, distinctive and spiritual, of which real events are only the symptoms or indeed the symbols, an effort must be made to influence the spiritual power that expresses itself in concrete things.[23]

And the means of influence must match the means by which the spiritual power expresses itself: 'Efforts were made to achieve real effects by means of symbolically significant action.'[24] For Weber, this symbolism is an expansion of magic which is 'transformed from a direct manipulation of forces into a *symbolic activity*'.[25]

Weber next discusses how various types of systematisation of the spiritual world – such as personifying the spiritual power and constructing a pantheon – may lead to a different, less magical attitude towards deities. This is a crucial development which distances this world from the spiritual one and brings with it the rise of priests and a new system of ethics. It is this development that Weber regards as being essentially religious.

It is, however, accompanied by the survival of magical religion, leading to 'the possibility of a dual relationship between men and the supernatural'.[26] In examining this dual relationship, Weber distinguishes between two different types of religious behaviour: magical and supplicatory. In the former, 'religious behaviour is not worship of the god but rather coercion of the god, and invocation is not prayer but rather the exercise of magical formulae'.[27] However, 'the boundary between magical formula and supplication remains fluid'.[28] And coercion is characteristic of both ancient and modern religions: 'Such magical coercion is universally diffused, and even the Catholic priest continues to practise something of this magical power in executing the miracle of the mass.'[29]

In addition to spoken ritual such as prayer, Weber identifies sacrifice as the second element in less magical religion. However, both elements have their origins in magic: 'Of course, the two characteristic elements of divine worship, prayer and sacrifice, have their origin in magic.'[30] The magical aspect of sacrifice stems from the fact that it is primarily concerned with offering something to a deity in the hope of receiving something back. In some cases this magical aspect has been diluted as a result of 'an increasing predominance of non-magical motives ... brought about by the growing recognition of the power of a god'.[31] Further dilution of the magical aspect in sacrifice and prayer depends on an increased concern with other-worldly rather than this-worldly ends, that is it depends on 'recession of the original, practical and calculating rationalism'[32] and 'systematisation of the god concept and of the thinking concerning the possible relationships of man to the divine'.[33]

Given such a dilution of the magical aspect, Weber is able to propose a distinction between magic and religion:

> The relationships of men to supernatural forces which take the forms of prayer, sacrifice and worship may be termed '*cult*' and '*religion*', as distinguished from '*sorcery*', which is magical coercion. Correspondingly, those beings that are worshipped and entreated religiously may be termed '*gods*', in contrast to '*demons*', which are magically coerced and charmed.[34]

However, he accepts that this distinction is an analytical construct that fails to provide an exact fit to the historical evidence: 'There may be no instance in which it is possible to apply this differentiation absolutely, since the cults we have just called "religious" practically everywhere contain numerous magical components.'[35]

Weber also distinguishes between magic and religion on other levels, principally in terms of different functionaries and different ethical systems. He suggests a distinction between self-employed magicians and cult-centred priests, but again concedes that applied to reality this difference is fluid: 'Even the theoretical *differentiae* of these types are not unequivocally determinable.'[36] The distinction between magical ethics, 'the ultimate warrant of which is taboo'[37] (with taboo referring to prohibitions applied to things considered to be impure), and religious ethics, sanctioned by fear of 'the ethical displeasure of the god',[38] is more straightforward. However, Weber again acknowledges that the historical evidence groups the two: 'In its early stages, the religious ethic consistently shares ... with magic worship in that it is frequently composed of a complex of heterogeneous prescriptions and prohibitions.'[39]

Elsewhere, in an article published in 1915, Weber provides a more general discussion of his views on religion and magic, arguing that religion gives meaning to social life while magic is concerned with more material ends. He describes later, less magical religion as legitimating success by relating it to divine favour and as providing a similar explanation for misfortune: 'In treating suffering as a symptom of odiousness in the eyes of the gods and as a sign of secret guilt, religion has psychologically met a very general need.'[40] Weber also discusses the question of theodicy, that is the task of accounting for evil and suffering when the divine is viewed as omnipotent and just, in particular of explaining misfortune that occurs to people regarded as innocent. He argues that, through accounts of the relationship between humans and deities that regard divine motives as being inaccessible to human understanding, religion gives 'rationally satisfactory answers to the questioning for the basis of the incongruity between destiny and merit'.[41] In contrast to such psychological or rational satisfactions, early religion – or any later religion still 'engulfed in the massive and archaic growth of magic'[42] – has more practical, this-worldly ends such as good health, prosperity and successful harvests.

Notes

1. Hegel 1984: 185.
2. Hegel 1987: 272.
3. Hegel 1984: 186.
4. Hegel 1984: 190.
5. Hegel 1984: 198.
6. Hegel 1987: 272.
7. Hegel 1987: 541.

8. Hegel 1985: 162.
9. Marx 1957: 42.
10. Marx 1957: 41.
11. Marx and Engels 1965: 42.
12. Engels 1957c: 281–2.
13. Engels 1957a: 146.
14. Engels 1957a: 147.
15. Engels 1957a: 147.
16. Engels 1957a: 147.
17. Engels 1957a: 147.
18. Engels 1957b: 225.
19. Engels 1957b: 225.
20. Engels 1957b: 225.
21. Weber 1978: 630.
22. Weber 1978: 402.
23. Weber 1978: 404.
24. Weber 1978: 405.
25. Weber 1978: 403.
26. Weber 1978: 419–20.
27. Weber 1978: 422.
28. Weber 1978: 422.
29. Weber 1978: 422.
30. Weber 1978: 422.
31. Weber 1978: 423.
32. Weber 1978: 424.
33. Weber 1978: 424.
34. Weber 1978: 424.
35. Weber 1978: 424.
36. Weber 1978: 425.
37. Weber 1978: 433.
38. Weber 1978: 437.
39. Weber 1978: 437.
40. Weber 1991a: 271.
41. Weber 1991a: 275.
42. Weber 1991a: 277.

2

.

Early intellectualist approaches

.

T HE THREE BRITISH SCHOLARS discussed in this chapter – Spencer, Tylor and Frazer – belong to the second half of the nineteenth century and their work therefore falls chronologically between that of Hegel and Weber discussed in the previous chapter. Like other nineteenth-century scholars, such as Hegel and Marx, Spencer and his colleagues regarded society as having developed through a regular sequence of stages. However, Spencer took a specifically evolutionist approach to social development, arguing that the biological theory of species evolution developed in the natural sciences can be applied outside those disciplines. Tylor and Frazer shared Spencer's assumptions but focused on cultural evolution, with culture being understood to cover such aspects of a society as its religion, customs and technology.

The three British scholars regarded this process of evolution less as a product of the dialectical law-like processes envisaged by Hegel and Marx, and more as following a general law of inevitable progress as individuals improve their knowledge of the world around them. Like Hegel they placed magic at the beginning of their evolutionist sequences; unlike Hegel, however, they regarded magic as distinct from religion. Their approach to religion is referred to specifically as intellectualist because they regarded religion as a means of explaining events by attributing them to divine agency and as owing its origin to people's attempts to explain aspects of the world around them. As one later anthropologist puts it, the intellectualist approach takes 'it for granted that primitive man was essentially rational, though his attempts to explain puzzling phenomena are crude and fallacious'.[1] This emphasis on religion as an explanatory model meant that the intellectualists introduced another method of explaining events – science – into their discussions of the sacred.

Spencer

Herbert Spencer (1820–96) was the major theorist of social evolution-ism, applying the principles of biological evolution to the evolution of human societies. He never attended university and, after some years' employment as a civil engineer and journalist, supported himself through his writing on the subject.

Spencer's theories are based on an analogy between society and an organism, which operates on two levels. On one level he thought that the biological theory of evolution, involving increasing complexity and differentiation of species, held true for the evolution of societies, enabling societies from different places and periods to be ranked in a temporal sequence based on the complexity of their social structures. On the second level he thought that, like an organism, a society con-sists of specialised, mutually dependent parts, such as religion, each functioning to maintain that society and meet its needs. This empha-sis on how a part maintains a whole contrasts with the type of social analysis presented by Marx and Weber, both of whom identified con-flicts of interest within societies. It was, however, influential on two twentieth-century schools of anthropological thought discussed in later chapters, both of which have somewhat clumsy titles.

One of these schools of thought, associated with Malinowski and discussed in the next chapter, is referred to as social-psychological functionalism, often abbreviated simply to functionalism, and inter-prets society as meeting human needs, from basic biological needs such as food to psychological needs such as the expression of emo-tions in group ceremonies like funeral rituals. The other school of thought, associated with Radcliffe-Brown and discussed in Chapter 5, is referred to as social-structural functionalism, often abbreviated to social structuralism or structural functionalism, and places more emphasis on a society's social structure and on how other aspects of a society contribute to the overall continuity of the social order.

Spencer's evolutionist theories are set forth in detail in his multi-volume *A System of Synthetic Philosophy*, published between 1862 and 1896, in the sixth volume of which he examines the origin and nature of magic and religion. He discusses magic in terms similar to those later made famous by Frazer as sympathetic magic. He describes magic as a particular trait of thought in oral societies, one in which 'the particular virtue possessed by an aggregate is supposed not only to inhere in all parts of it, but to extend to whatever is associated with it'.[2] Thus a magician 'begins by obtaining a part of his victim's body, or something closely associated with his body, or else by making a representation of him',[3] and then 'he does to this part, or this representation, something which he thinks is thereby done to his victim'.[4] Spencer argues that the beliefs behind such actions stem from false speculation, based on an incorrect assessment of objects and their relations which is only corrected 'as knowledge advances and observation becomes critical'.[5]

According to Spencer, religion also originated in false speculation, in this case attempts to explain phenomena such as dreams. Such speculation led to a concept of people having a double which survives death and appears in dreams as a ghost, the first supernatural being: 'The first traceable conception of a supernatural being is the conception of a ghost.'[6] The concept of ghosts then developed into the concept of deities: 'By transition from the dream to the ghost, and from the ghost to the god, there is reached a conceived kind of cause capable of indefinite expansion.'[7] While a belief in such supernatural agents constitutes one aspect of religion, the other is a practice of worshipping them: 'Using the phrase ancestor-worship in its broadest sense as comprehending all worship of the dead ... we conclude that ancestor-worship is the root of every religion.'[8] In addition, Spencer argues that magic adapted to the coming of religion, with the magician's methods developing from 'the simpler form of magic to the form in which supernatural agents are employed'.[9]

Tylor

E. B. Tylor (1832–1917) is regarded as the European founder of anthropology, as influential in his discipline as Weber and Durkheim were in theirs. Like Spencer, he did not attend university, working instead as a businessman while pursuing his interest in the culture of oral societies. In 1884, however, Oxford University created a readership in anthropology for him and two years later he became the first professor in the discipline.

While Tylor's concern was what he defined as culture, he shared Spencer's interest in the evolution of societies and was similarly confident that he could arrange them in sequence. To Spencer's social evolutionism he added the idea of survivals: forms of behaviour which he regarded as having been carried over from earlier stages in a society's development. Thus, according to Tylor, evidence for the early stages in cultural evolution can be drawn both from oral societies and from the parts of modern societies that constitute survivals. His best known work is *Primitive Culture*, published in 1871, in which he applies his theories to the evolution of religion and magic and describes survivals as 'fragments of a dead lower culture embedded in a living higher one'.[10]

Magic, which Tylor describes as a false or occult science, 'one of the most pernicious delusions that ever vexed mankind',[11] represents such a survival. It 'belongs in its main principle to the lowest known stages of civilization'[12] but has 'lasted on more or less among modern cultured nations'.[13] For Tylor, like Spencer, magic came into being through intellectual error. It is 'a sincere but fallacious system of philosophy'[14] arising from 'man ... mistaking an ideal for a real connexion',[15] with the ideal connection taking the form of contiguity or 'of mere analogy or symbolism'.[16]

Religion also originated in intellectual error, although Tylor's reconstruction of the thought-processes behind its origin is more difficult to summarise. Part of his emphasis is on the concept of the human soul as an explanation of, for example, the difference between a living and a dead body, a deduction 'answering in the most forcible way to the plain evidence of man's senses, as interpreted by a fairly consistent and rational primitive philosophy'.[17] Tylor argues that in a further step of reasoning people thought that souls were able to enter physical objects. This belief that objects have souls, referred to as animism, is not restricted to oral societies: 'Animism characterises tribes very low in the scale of humanity, and thence ascends, deeply modified in its transmission, but from first to last preserving an unbroken continuity, into the midst of high modern culture.'[18] His definition of religion is more straightforward and is the one most frequently used in anthropology. He suggests 'as a minimum definition of religion, the belief in spiritual beings'[19] and, like Spencer, regards worship as the primary religious practice. For Tylor the belief in souls has provided the basis for all subsequent religions:

> It seems as though the conception of a human soul, when once attained to by man, served as a type of model on which he framed not only his ideas of other souls of lower grade, but also his ideas of spiritual beings in general.[20]

Frazer
·

J. G. Frazer (1854–1941) began his academic life as a classicist but, partly as a result of reading Tylor's work, became increasingly interested in anthropology. He studied at Glasgow University before moving to Cambridge University, where he spent most of his long career. He is most famous for *The Golden Bough*, first published in two volumes in 1890, whose primary focus is on the evidence in a wide range of societies for what he refers to as sacred kingship. Frazer constantly compiled new material for *The Golden Bough*, adding classical and Biblical myths as well as folklore from other periods and places, resulting in its republication in twelve volumes between 1907 and 1915. A one-volume abridged edition was published in 1922 and it is on this edition that the following discussion concentrates. While the evolutionist aspects of *The Golden Bough* belong to the nineteenth century, the book's long publication history, and popularity, carried its influence into the beginning of the twentieth century.

In *The Golden Bough* Frazer examines two particular aspects of sacred kingship. One is the relationship between a sacred king and his subjects, in which the subjects regard their well-being as dependent on the well-being of the king because he is identified with cosmic forces or thought to have control over them, including such economically important natural forces as rainfall. The other related aspect is the ritual killing of such kings when their power diminishes, because this physical decline is regarded as causing a parallel weakening in his control over or identification with cosmic forces. This discussion of sacred kingship takes place within an evolutionist framework that owes much to Tylor's work except that, while Tylor saw magic and religion as co-existing to varying degrees in the different stages of all societies, Frazer tends to place the two in a more emphatic evolutionary sequence. Like Tylor, however, Frazer compares magic with science, which he regards as the highest stage in cultural evolution.

Frazer describes magic as 'the bastard sister of science',[21] arising from 'one great disastrous fallacy, a mistaken conception of the association of ideas'.[22] He characterises taboos – the prohibitions applied to things thought to be impure – as the negative side of magic, and sorcery as its positive side, and distinguishes between two different principles of thought on which a sorcerer's sympathetic magic is based. The first is homeopathic magic obeying the law of similarity: 'Like produces like.'[23] The second is contagious magic obeying the law of contact: 'Things which have once been in contact with each other continue to act on each other at a distance.'[24] Magic, for Frazer, is thus an attempt to control events through the application of these laws, both of which he regards as being based on an erroneous theory of causality.

According to Frazer, all early societies believed in magic, with some moving on to religion: 'The former represents a ruder and earlier phase of the human mind, through which all the races of mankind have passed or are passing on their way to religion.'[25] He explains the passage to religion in terms of some individuals realising the inefficacy of magic and seeking a different means of explaining events that occur in the natural world:

> If the great world went on its way without the help of him or his fellows, it must surely be because there were other beings, like himself, but far stronger, who, unseen themselves, directed its course and brought about all the varied series of events which he had hitherto believed to be dependent on his own magic.[26]

This emphasis on religion as giving meaning to the natural world contrasts with Weber's view of religion as giving meaning to the social world.

Frazer's concept of unseen other beings is central to his definition of religion which he regards as consisting of two elements: 'A belief in powers higher than man and an attempt to propitiate or please them.'[27] As religion assumes the world to be directed by higher powers who may be turned from their purpose, that is it regards deities as addressable beings, it is 'directly opposed to the principles of magic as well as of science, both of which assume that the processes of nature are rigid and invariable in their operation'.[28]

However, Frazer accepts that sometimes distinguishing between magic and religion can be difficult because 'magic often deals with spirits, which are personal agents of the kind assumed by religion'.[29] Here, instead, a distinction between different attitudes to the spirits has to be made, with magic treating 'them exactly in the same fashion as it treats inanimate agents, that is, it constrains or coerces instead of conciliating or propitiating them as religion would do'.[30] According to Frazer, such a combination of magical coercion with a religious belief in spirits – what he refers to as a 'confusion of ideas, the same mixture of religion and magic'[31] – is to be found in the fertility ritual known as sacred marriage. This ritual involves the marriage of vegetation deities or their representatives 'to ensure the fruitfulness of the earth',[32] while related rituals involving the death and revival of such deities mirror the progress of the seasons. As Frazer puts it, people began by imagining that they could 'hasten or retard the flight of the seasons by magic art'[33] but later 'explained the fluctuations of growth and decay ... by the marriage, the death, and the rebirth or revival of the gods'.[34] Thus, according to Frazer, 'a religious theory was blended with a magical practice'.[35]

The change from religion to science, the highest stage reached so far in cultural evolution, is also explained by Frazer in terms of new explanatory models being sought. Religion was discovered to represent an unsatisfactory explanation because 'it assumes that the succession of natural events is not determined by immutable laws ... and this assumption is not borne out by closer observation'.[36] Therefore 'religion, regarded as an explanation of nature, is displaced by science'.[37]

Notes

1. Evans-Pritchard 1965: 20.
2. Spencer 1885: 242.
3. Spencer 1885: 243.
4. Spencer 1885: 243.
5. Spencer 1885: 101.
6. Spencer 1885: 281.
7. Spencer 1885: 772.
8. Spencer 1885: 411.
9. Spencer 1885: 243.
10. Tylor 1929a: 72.
11. Tylor 1929a: 112.
12. Tylor 1929a: 112.
13. Tylor 1929a: 112.
14. Tylor 1929a: 134.
15. Tylor 1929a: 116.
16. Tylor 1929a: 117.
17. Tylor 1929a: 429.
18. Tylor 1929a: 426.
19. Tylor 1929a: 424.
20. Tylor 1929b: 110.
21. Frazer 1990: 50.
22. Frazer 1990: 20.
23. Frazer 1990: 11.
24. Frazer 1990: 11.
25. Frazer 1990: 56.

26. Frazer 1990: 58.
27. Frazer 1990: 50.
28. Frazer 1990: 51.
29. Frazer 1990: 51.
30. Frazer 1990: 51.
31. Frazer 1990: 53.
32. Frazer 1990: 136.
33. Frazer 1990: 324.
34. Frazer 1990: 324.
35. Frazer 1990: 324.
36. Frazer 1990: 711.
37. Frazer 1990: 712.

3
·

Emotionalist approaches

·

THE THREE SCHOLARS DISCUSSED in this chapter, Marett, Freud and Malinowski, developed an emotionalist interpretation of religion and magic, regarding them as a response to stressful emotions rather than, as the intellectualists argued, as an intellectual response to otherwise inexplicable events. While this shared perception of magic and, to a lesser degree, religion enables the three scholars to be grouped together, their wider theoretical perspectives differed. Marett was an anthropologist who brought a new approach to the study of the sacred in oral societies while continuing the intellectualist tradition of gathering data from various societies. Freud was a psychologist whose studies of religion were much influenced by the intellectualists but whose interpretation of religion emphasised the role of his primary concern, the unconscious mind. Just as Freud's interest in the unconscious transformed psychology, so Malinowski transformed his discipline of anthropology, turning it from the type of armchair comparative studies favoured by the intellectualists to fieldwork and the study of individual societies for their own qualities.

Marett
·

R. R. Marett (1866–1943) was an English anthropologist who, like his contemporary Frazer, brought to anthropology a background in classical literature. He studied at Oxford University where, from 1891 until his death, he held various positions, including reader in anthropology from 1910 to 1936. He shared the intellectualists' interest in identifying the origins of religion and magic and of charting their subsequent development. However, his interpretation of magic and religion differed from theirs: he interpreted magic in emotionalist terms as a response to stress, while developing a different, more descriptive approach to religion which placed particular emphasis on the nature of religious experience and feelings. This interest in the nature of religious consciousness resembles the type of approach to the sacred taken by certain Continental scholars, an approach referred to as phenomenological and discussed in the next chapter.

In an article published in 1900 Marett argues that religion in oral societies is primarily a question of feeling rather than of thought and that such feelings remain characteristic of religion in literate societies. In particular he refers to the feeling of awe: 'Of all the English words awe is, I think, the one that most expresses the fundamental religious feeling most nearly.'[1] This awe is not simply fear of the divine but a compound of feelings also involving wonder, admiration and love. Marett suggests that such awe may have been a response to concepts more impersonal than Tylor's souls and therefore that a pre-animistic stage may have existed in the development of religion. Subsequent religious development, according to Marett, has depended on refinements in the emotional response to the divine, for example feelings of reverence and of humility, and on a more reflective attitude emerging towards the divine.

In an article published in 1904 Marett associates a different type of feeling with magic, arguing that it arises from the emotion of tension and is cathartic or stimulating, providing relief or encouragement when technical methods are inadequate. As he puts it in relation to catharsis: 'To work off one's wrath on any apology for an enemy is expletive, that is cathartic.'[2] He regards magic as 'a more or less clearly-recognised pretending, which at the same time is believed to project itself into an ulterior effect'.[3] He suggests that this belief is less to do with a false association of ideas, as intellectualists argue, and more to do with 'a projection of imperative will ... that moves on a supernatural plane'.[4] However, in an article published in 1909, Marett suggests that a closer relationship exists between magic and religion. He argues that the supernatural plane of magic and the impersonal, pre-animistic power evoking awe are similar, concluding that 'much of what has hitherto been classed as magic ... is really religion of an elementary kind'.[5] He suggests further that magic and religion arose from the same source and in view of this, and of the problem of distinguishing between the two, he prefers to use the term magico-religious to describe the early stages in the development of both.

Freud and psychoanalysis
.

The Austrian psychologist Sigmund Freud (1856–1939) discussed religion in very different terms to those used by Marett. He regarded religion as a particular type of emotionally disturbed adult behaviour, caused by unpleasant or traumatic childhood experiences forgotten in the conscious part of the mind and repressed in the unconscious. Freud's account of religion thus differs from Marett's not only in terms of the emotions involved but in that Marett sought to describe religion while Freud tried to explain it.

Psychology, the study of the mind and of its effect on human behaviour, that is of how people think and what causes their actions, was only established as a separate academic discipline in the nineteenth century, previously being incorporated within other disciplines such as theology and philosophy. It was radically transformed by Freud's work which stressed the influence of the unconscious on human behaviour. Much of the early work in psychology had concentrated on what might be termed normal behaviour. Freud, however, was one of the first scholars to offer a system of psychology that, through its emphasis on the unconscious, took account of abnormal as well as normal behaviour. The school of psychology that he founded is referred to as psychoanalysis, concerned both with the study of mentally and emotionally disturbed behaviour and the treatment of such behaviour.

Freud studied medicine at Vienna University before working in that city's general hospital. In 1886 he went into private practice, developing his psychoanalytic theories and techniques. He faced much opposition to his work during his lifetime but did receive some academic recognition, being given the title of professor by Vienna University in 1902. The last years of his life coincided with the rise to power of Hitler and when the German army arrived in Austria in 1938 he and his family moved to London where he died one year later. Much of the opposition to Freud's work, both in his lifetime and since, relates to the radical nature of psychoanalysis: its insistence that the unconscious plays a more important role in motivating human behaviour than had previously been acknowledged; that much adult mental illness, referred to as neurotic and involving such symptoms as anxiety and obsessive behaviour, is caused by traumatic childhood experiences, often of a sexual nature; and that such illness should be treated by free association, that is encouraging the patient to express emotions, thoughts and memories spontaneously, enabling the analyst to identify the unconscious cause of the illness.

The particular childhood trauma that Freud associated with religion is of a sexual nature. According to Freud, a boy's first sexual feelings are directed towards his mother, accompanied by jealousy towards the father. This jealousy is ambivalent, with the boy both admiring his father's sexual role and wanting to replace him, and is followed by feelings of guilt. These emotions are referred to as the Oedipus complex, named after the classical Greek tragedy in which Oedipus unwittingly kills his father and marries his mother. According to Freud, these childhood traumas are repressed in the unconscious and lie behind adult beliefs in deities who represent a kind of magnified version of this original complex of emotions focusing on the father.

Freud also believed that the stages in childhood development correspond to stages in cultural evolution and that magic as well as religion can be interpreted in psychoanalytic terms, with magic preceding the religious complex of emotions in the history of both an individual and society. These various ideas are set forth in *Totem and Taboo*, published in 1913, in which Freud adapts much of the evolutionary framework of the intellectualists into a psychoanalytic scheme.

In this book Freud broadly follows Tylor's evolutionary sequence, identifying 'an animistic phase followed by a religious phase and this in turn by a scientific one'.[6] He associates two techniques with animism – sorcery and magic – defining sorcery as 'the art of influencing spirits by treating them in the same way as one would treat men in like circumstances',[7] and magic as 'something different: fundamentally, it disregards spirits and makes use of special procedures and not of everyday psychological methods'.[8] Moreover, magic preceded sorcery: 'It is easy to guess that magic is the earlier and more important branch of animistic technique.'[9] He argues further that an earlier type of magic preceded animism: 'The assumptions of magic are more fundamental and older than the doctrine of spirits, which forms the kernel of animism.'[10] He equates this earlier type of magic with the pre-animism proposed by Marett, but which Marett regarded as religious.

Freud's acceptance of Tylor's description of the basis of magic is more straightforward: 'Tylor ... states it in its most succinct form as mistaking an ideal connection for a real one.'[11] Similarly, Freud accepts Frazer's distinction between homeopathic and contagious magic: 'Similarity and contiguity are the two essential principles of processes of association.'[12] However, he thinks the intellectualist approach of Tylor and Frazer is limited and fails to identify magic's hidden motive. Like Marett, he finds this motive in the proposal that 'primitive man had an immense belief in the power of his wishes'.[13]

In psychoanalytic terms the magical stage in cultural evolution can be described as narcissistic, that is as characterised by love of self. Freud suggests further that the stages in cultural evolution parallel the stages in a child's sexual or libidinal development: 'We are encouraged to attempt a comparison between the phases in the development of men's view of the universe and the stages of an individual's libidinal development.'[14] Thus magic corresponds to a child's narcissistic stage: 'This kind of representation of a satisfied wish is quite comparable to children's play.'[15] Moreover, this narcissism can re-emerge in mentally ill adults: 'The omnipotence of thoughts, the overvaluation of mental processes as compared with reality, is seen to have unrestricted play in the emotional life of neurotic patients.'[16]

Freud also rejects Frazer's suggestion that religion originated in people realising that magic represents an inadequate explanatory model: 'It can scarcely have been a recognition of the falseness of his premises, for he continued to practise the magical technique.'[17] Instead Freud argues that religion's origin lay in an enactment of the Oedipus complex which he relates to totemism, the worship of animals and plants associated with particular social groups. He argues that 'the totem animal is in reality a substitute for the father'.[18] More specifically, it is a substitute for an earlier father who had monopolised all the social group's women and had been killed by his sons. The two principal rules associated with totemism – not to kill the totem and to marry outside one's community – arose from the sons' subsequent guilt: 'They revoked their deed by forbidding the killing of the totem, the substitute for their father; and they renounced its fruits by resigning their claim to the women.'[19] These rules underlie all subsequent religions: 'Totemic religion arose from the filial sense of guilt, in an attempt to allay that feeling and to appease the father by deferred obedience to him. All later religions are seen to be attempts at solving the same problem.'[20]

The religious stage in cultural evolution, initiated by this early murder, is described in psychoanalytic terms as one of object choice, that is when self-love develops into love of another person. As for magic, Freud suggests that this stage corresponds to a stage in the individual's development: 'The religious phase would correspond to the stage of object-choice of which the characteristic is a child's attachment to his parents.'[21] Bringing his evolutionary sequence to a close, Freud describes the scientific stage in cultural evolution as an acceptance of reality. Again this corresponds to a stage in the individual's development: 'The scientific phase would have an exact counterpart in the stage at which an individual has reached maturity.'[22]

Malinowski and functionalism

.

The influence of Bronislaw Malinowski (1884–1942) on his discipline of anthropology was in many ways as radical as Freud's on psychology. Malinowski was born in Poland and studied in universities in Cracow and Leipzig. Having become increasingly interested in anthropology, partly through the influence of Frazer's *The Golden Bough*, in 1910 he began studying at the London School of Economics where anthropology had recently been established as a discipline. He subsequently spent several years on extensive fieldwork, including periods on the Trobriand Islands in the south-west Pacific during the First World War, a research position organised with the assistance of Marett. Not long after the end of the war he began lecturing at the London School of Economics where he was appointed professor of anthropology in 1927, a position from which he became the dominant figure in British anthropology. He moved to the United States in 1938 where he was appointed professor of anthropology at Yale University.

Malinowski's fieldwork, with its emphasis on what is referred to as participant observation, represents one of his major contributions to anthropology, turning the discipline from armchair scholarship to firsthand observation of oral societies. Partly as a result of this emphasis on fieldwork another major change occurred: interest switched to the study of specific societies for their own qualities rather than for their assumed relation to stages in a reconstructed evolutionary sequence. However, while Malinowski rejected the type of evolutionist approach favoured by scholars such as Spencer, he adopted a modified version of that scholar's analogy between a society and an organism.

Malinowski agreed with Spencer that societies are integrated wholes consisting of indispensable parts each fulfilling a function, but he argued that these functions are primarily directed towards meeting an individual's biological and emotional needs. This type of approach, now referred to as functionalism, put Malinowski in opposition to a different modification of Spencer's theories, referred to as structural functionalism and discussed in Chapter 5, which emphasises a society's collective concerns rather than the individual's needs and argues that parts of a society are not simply mutually dependent but also are similarly structured.

While Malinowski was primarily interested in using fieldwork to study specific societies he also addressed the more general questions of the nature of religion and magic, in particular in an article pub-

lished in 1925 which also illustrates his emphasis on the individual's
needs and his opposition to social evolutionism. He begins this article
by rejecting the evolutionist hypothesis that magic, religion and
science can be arranged in sequence, arguing that they are present in
all societies: 'There are no peoples however primitive without religion
and magic. Nor are there, it must be added at once, any savage races
lacking either in the scientific attitude or in science.'[23] Instead he
regards science, given a broad meaning incorporating commonsense
and technology, as existing in tandem with magic rather than being a
later substitute for it. Thus he points to a complementary relationship
between science and magic in practical activities:

> In his relation to nature and destiny, whether he tries to exploit the first
> or to dodge the second, primitive man recognises both the natural and the
> supernatural forces and agencies, and he tries to use them both for his
> benefit.[24]

He argues similarly that 'primitive man ... never relies on magic
alone',[25] but instead 'he clings to it, whenever he has to recognise the
impotence of his knowledge'.[26]

This complementary relationship between magic and science
relates to Malinowski's distinction between magic, through which
ends are achieved, and religion, in which ends are achieved. He
defines 'magic as a practical art consisting of acts which are only
means to a definite end expected to follow later on; religion as a
body of self-contained acts being themselves the fulfilment of their
purpose'.[27] Similarly, while both magic and religion 'arise and function in situations of emotional stress',[28] magic is primarily practical
and religion primarily expressive.

Like Marett, Malinowski suggests that magic arises in situations of
stress in which technical methods are insufficient to achieve desired
ends, with magic releasing such stress in rituals that imitate and
further the desired ends. As he puts it: 'Man, engaged in a series of
practical activities, comes to a gap ... His nervous system and his
whole organism drive him to some substitute activity.'[29] Magic is
thus, for example in a ritual to prevent death in childbirth, 'a means
to an end, it has a definite practical purpose which is known to all
who practise it'.[30] Similarly, he regards fertility rituals as 'acts of
magical nature, by which plenty is brought about',[31] and totemism,
the worship of animals and plants discussed by Freud as the earliest
religion, as a magical attempt to impose control on a basic biological
need, the 'living larder'.[32]

While Malinowski's interpretation of magic is similar to Marett's, his interpretation of religion differs. He associates religion with stress created by life's critical situations, with religion relieving such stress in rituals that are primarily expressive. For example, a ritual celebrating a birth is not a means to an end but an end in itself: 'It expresses the feelings of the mother, father, the relatives, the whole community, but there is no future event which this ceremony foreshadows, which it is meant to bring about or to prevent.'[33] Malinowski supports this interpretation by offering further examples of what he regards as religion. These include initiation and marriage rituals in which 'the ceremony and its purpose are one ... the end is realised in the very consummation of the event',[34] and sacrifice interpreted as expressing gratitude for providence and making sacred 'the great value of food'.[35] Funeral rituals are similarly religious: 'We find self-contained acts, the aim of which is achieved in their very performance. The ritual despair, the obsequies, the acts of mourning, express the emotion of the bereaved and the loss of the whole group.'[36] The emotions aroused by death, particularly fear, also explain the origin of the concept of immortality: 'The belief in immortality is the result of a deep emotional revelation, standardised by religion.'[37]

The concept of immortality also provides Malinowski with an argument against structural functionalism which he regards as underestimating the importance of the individual and overstating religion's social role. As he puts it with regard to immortality:

> The saving belief in spiritual continuity after death is already contained in the individual mind; it is not created by society. The sum total of innate tendencies, known usually as 'the instinct of self-preservation', is at the root of this belief.[38]

Similarly he argues: 'The fact is that the social share in religious enactment is a condition necessary but not sufficient, and that without the analysis of the individual mind, we cannot take one step in the understanding of religion.'[39]

Notes

1. Marett 1914a: 13.
2. Marett 1914b: 44.
3. Marett 1914b: 48.
4. Marett 1914b: 51.

5. Marett 1914c: xxi.
6. Freud 1985a: 146.
7. Freud 1985a: 135.
8. Freud 1985a: 135.
9. Freud 1985a: 135–6.
10. Freud 1985a: 150.
11. Freud 1985a: 136.
12. Freud 1985a: 140.
13. Freud 1985a: 141.
14. Freud 1985a: 148.
15. Freud 1985a: 141.
16. Freud 1985a: 145.
17. Freud 1985a: 151.
18. Freud 1985a: 202.
19. Freud 1985a: 205.
20. Freud 1985a: 206.
21. Freud 1985a: 148.
22. Freud 1985a: 148.
23. Malinowski 1982a: 17.
24. Malinowski 1982a: 32.
25. Malinowski 1982a: 32.
26. Malinowski 1982a: 32.
27. Malinowski 1982a: 88.
28. Malinowski 1982a: 87.
29. Malinowski 1982a: 79.
30. Malinowski 1982a: 37–8.
31. Malinowski 1982a: 46.
32. Malinowski 1982a: 44.
33. Malinowski 1982a: 38.
34. Malinowski 1982a: 40.
35. Malinowski 1982a: 42.
36. Malinowski 1982a: 52.
37. Malinowski 1982a: 51.
38. Malinowski 1982a: 62.
39. Malinowski 1982a: 69.

4
·

Phenomenological approaches

·

W HILE MARETT'S ATTEMPT TO describe the religious experience
represents an isolated strand in anthropology, such descriptions
are central to phenomenological approaches to the sacred. Phenomenology, a term already encountered in the discussion of Hegel's
work, is concerned with the study of phenomena, that is objects as
they are experienced rather than the objects themselves. Reflecting
this emphasis, phenomenology is often said to be a descriptive philosophy of experience, aiming to describe precisely the contents of consciousness. Phenomenology was founded by the German philosopher
Edmund Husserl (1859–1938) who argued that various steps have to
be taken in order to describe the contents of consciousness accurately.
These steps include what he referred to as eliminating or bracketing
off both the object experienced and the non-essential aspects of that
experience, so that what remains is the essential aspects of the experience. Husserl also argued that to achieve an accurate description all
assumptions and presuppositions have to be set aside. Thus phenomenology aims to provide a neutral description of the experience of an
object rather than to judge the validity of that experience or explain
what causes it.

With the exception of Marett's description of awe as characterising
the religious experience, phenomenology has largely been rejected by
anthropologists as a method of studying the sacred. However, it has
found more favour with historians of religion such as Otto and Eliade
whose work is discussed in this chapter. Both these scholars concentrated on describing the main features in the experience of religious
persons. In doing so, they placed more emphasis than other scholars
on the source of those experiences, that is on what Hegel referred to

as the object that is in religion: in Otto's term the numinous, in Eliade's the sacred. Because Jung's approach to religion, based on analytical psychology, is in some ways similar to those of Otto and Eliade, his theories are also discussed in this chapter. Phenomenology continues to influence contemporary historians of religion and the chapter ends by discussing a recent study, written by Smart, which takes such an approach.

Otto
.

Rudolf Otto (1869–1937), the German theologian, philosopher and historian of religions, studied theology and philosophy at the Universities of Erlangen and Göttingen. In 1904 he was appointed professor of theology at Göttingen, subsequently moving in 1914 to Breslau University and in 1917 to Marburg University where he taught until his retirement. His best known work is *The Idea of the Holy*, published in 1917, which Husserl, his contemporary at Göttingen University, hailed as a masterly application of the phenomenological method to religion.

In *The Idea of the Holy* Otto continues the nineteenth-century interest in cultural development. However, he replaces the intellectualist emphasis on religion as an explanatory model with an emphasis on religious consciousness, associating different stages in his developmental sequence with a different range of magico-religious feelings. He thus describes the change from magic to religion in terms of a wider range of feelings being experienced rather than as a search for a better explanatory model.

Otto begins *The Idea of the Holy* by arguing that the term holy embraces two aspects of religion, one apprehensible and the other mysterious. The apprehensible elements of religion are those, such as questions of morality and divine purpose, which can be discussed in rational terms. His interest in this book is in the mysterious aspect of religion which he regards as more fundamental and refers to as the numinous, from the Latin *numen* meaning divine power. While the numinous cannot be discussed in rational terms, he suggests that it can be described in terms of how it is experienced: 'The nature of the numinous can only be suggested by means of the special way in which it is reflected in the mind in terms of feeling.'[1]

He describes the full religious experience, again using Latin terminology, as one of *mysterium tremendum et fascinans*. *Mysterium* points to the mysterious, or wholly other, character of the divine; *tremendum*

33

points to the awfulness bordering on dread experienced in confronting the divine, a feeling which Otto compares to the awe proposed by Marett as the identifying characteristic of religion; and *fascinans* points to the attraction felt for the divine, an attraction associated with rapture and love. This range of feelings provides a framework within which Otto can order different magico-religious phenomena, that is different experiences of the numinous drawn from various societies.

He regards everyone as having an innate predisposition, a 'faculty of *divination*',[2] capable of experiencing the numinous. However, this predisposition has only been fully awakened over the course of religious development: 'The numinous only unfolds its full content by slow degrees, as one by one the series of requisite stimuli or incitements becomes operative.'[3] He regards religious development as having begun with magic: 'The magical is nothing but a suppressed and dimmed form of the numinous.'[4] He distinguishes between an early magic seeking to influence events through principles similar to those of Frazer's sympathetic magic and a later magic in which events are attributed to 'certain definite operations of force'[5] characterised as demoniac. The feeling evoked by these demons is one of awfulness and thus magic represents a form of proto-religion, it is 'the vestibule at the threshold of the real religious feeling, an earliest stirring of the numinous consciousness'.[6]

Otto's argument about how this limited experience of the numinous has developed into what he regards as a full experience is complex. Partly his argument is that certain thought-processes were applied to the phenomena of religious experience so that they acquired more rational and moral characteristics. And partly his argument is that the previously mentioned stimuli or incitements have aroused a fuller experience of the numinous. In terms of the development of Christianity he suggests that the Biblical prophets, and in particular the figure of Christ, were such stimuli. For Otto, as for Hegel, it is Christianity, which he regards as the fullest experience of the numinous, that constitutes the culminating stage in the development of religion.

Jung and analytical psychology

Carl Jung (1875–1961), the Swiss psychologist, studied medicine and other subjects at Basel and Zurich Universities. On finishing his studies in 1902 he established his own research practice in mental illness, working in collaboration with Freud. About ten years later, he broke away from Freud's influence, rejecting the latter's emphasis on the sexual basis of neuroses and developing his own school of psychology, referred to as analytical psychology. Following Jung's break with Freud much of his research focused on a part of the mind, discussed further below, that he called the collective unconscious. He believed this collective unconscious was of fundamental importance to the study of religion which he defined in terms taken from Otto. In his later years he received academic recognition for his work, becoming professor of psychology at Zurich University in 1933 and then at Basel University in 1943.

Jung's rejection of Freud's emphasis on the sexual basis of neurosis, that is Freud's view that emotionally disturbed or neurotic behaviour is a consequence of childhood sexual traumas, had implications for Jung's analysis of religion. While Freud regarded religion as an instance of neurotic behaviour and related it to childhood emotions repressed in the unconscious, Jung regarded religion as essential to achieving self-fulfilment and related it to the collective unconscious, a part of the mind inherited by each individual which contains the collective experiences of that individual's ancestors. More specifically, Jung regarded the collective unconscious as containing what he referred to as archetypes: mental models that generate specific magico-religious images and myths whose similarities relate to their collective nature.

In a lecture delivered in 1937 Jung used Otto's term numinous to define religion:

> Religion, as the Latin word denotes [*religare* means to bind], is a careful and scrupulous observation of what Rudolf Otto aptly termed the *numinosum*, that is, a dynamic agency or effect not caused by an arbitrary act of will. On the contrary, it seizes and controls the human subject, who is always rather its victim than its creator.[7]

However, Jung rejected Otto's description of magic as a limited experience of the numinous, suggesting instead that magic is coercive: 'A great many ritualistic performances are carried out for the sole purpose of producing at will the effect of the *numinosum* by means of certain devices of a magical nature.'[8] Also unlike Otto, he related experience of the numinous not to an individual's innate predisposition towards such an experience but to the collective unconscious and its 'authentic religious function'.[9] In Jung's terms, the experience of the numinous is the experience of the archetypes in the collective unconscious.

In a lecture delivered in 1934, Jung discussed the concept of the collective unconscious in more detail: 'The collective unconscious ... does not ... owe its existence to personal experience but exclusively to heredity.'[10] He described the contents of the collective unconscious as archetypes: 'The concept of the archetype, which is an indispensable correlate of the collective unconscious, indicates the existence of definite forms in the psyche which seem to be present always and everywhere.'[11] These archetypes are *forms without content*, representing merely the possibility of a certain type of perception and action'.[12] He suggested that different archetypal forms generate different sets of magical and religious images, such as the magical images of witches and the religious images of goddesses generated by the anima-archetype, a term derived from the word's original meaning of soul or spirit and used by Jung to represent the feminine side of a man's nature.

According to Jung, the archetypal forms also contain the recurrent themes and patterns of myth and ritual which he regarded as essential to individuation, a process through which individuals can reach self-fulfilment. He argued that myths and magico-religious images help achieve individuation in various ways, by resolving any contradictions in one's sense of self, by preparing the individual to face situations in life and by bringing forth the possibilities latent in the collective unconscious. For example, to return to the anima-archetype in men, he suggested that this feminine element in the unconscious prepares men for the experience of women and makes a loving relationship with a woman possible. The animus-archetype, Jung's term for the masculine element in the female unconscious, performs a similar function in and for women.

In an article published in 1934, Jung argues that magic and religion have declined in our society. Because they aid individuation, this decline is harmful: 'Our intellect has achieved the most tremendous things, but in the meantime our spiritual dwelling has fallen into disrepair.'[13] While he suggests that to some extent this disrepair can be remedied through the principles and practices of analytical psychology, he argues that members of oral societies are better balanced psychologically because they assimilate 'all outer sense experiences to inner, psychic events'.[14] A similar distinction is stressed by Jung in an article published in 1931: 'The primary assumptions of archaic man are essentially different from ours, so that he lives in a different world.'[15]

Eliade
•

The influence of both Jung and phenomenology is evident in much of the work of the Romanian scholar Mircea Eliade (1907–86) who studied philosophy at Bucharest University and then Indian philosophy at Calcutta University. Between 1933 and 1939 he was assistant professor at the former university where he taught Indian philosophy and the history of religions. After the end of the Second World War in 1945, he emigrated to France, becoming professor in the history of religions at the Sorbonne, part of the University of Paris, and attending a series of annual conferences hosted by Jung in Switzerland. Having moved to the United States, he became professor at the University of Chicago in 1956.

Eliade is perhaps best known for a distinction he proposed between religions in which time is experienced in cyclic terms, with ritual regularly re-enacting the original actions of deities that serve as models for subsequent human behaviour, and religions such as Christianity in which time is experienced in linear or historical terms. However, many of Eliade's studies of religion reveal a clearer debt to the work of both Otto and Jung. While his conclusions were often similar to Jung's, he followed Otto in relating the religious experience to the divine, substituting the term 'sacred' for Otto's numinous and using it to include both magic and religion.

An example of Jung's influence on Eliade is provided by *Patterns in Comparative Religion* which was published in 1949. Eliade's approach in this book is similar to Jung's method of postulating archetypal forms on the basis of similarities between various images and myths found in different societies. However, Eliade refers to hierophanies, that is revelations or manifestations of the sacred in nature, rather than to images and myths generated by the collective unconscious. And he groups these hierophanies into patterns or symbolic systems rather than into archetypal forms, on the basis that each pattern represents 'a coherent collection of common traits'.[16]

Having identified these patterns, Eliade describes the essential experiences they represent, arguing that these experiences help to resolve life's critical situations, in much the same way as Jung argued that myths aid successful individuation. For example, Eliade describes what he regards as various lunar hierophanies, such as the moon itself in various images, floods, the growth and decay of vegetation, the snake that sheds its skin, and the bear that appears and disappears with the seasons. These belong to a pattern he refers to as 'moon-rain-fertility-woman-serpent-death-periodic-regeneration'.[17] This pattern reveals what Eliade characterises as 'the law of becoming, and no change is final; every change is merely part of a cyclic pattern'.[18] He argues that as such the pattern helps people come to terms with their own mortality. For Eliade it is irrelevant whether the hierophanies in the patterns are magical or religious. As he comments in discussing lunar hierophanies: 'All the values of the moon, whether cosmological, magic or religious, are explained by its modality of *being*; by the fact that it is "living", and inexhaustible in its own regeneration.'[19]

Eliade thinks that members of earlier societies experienced the pattern or symbolic system behind each hierophany: 'The primitive mind did genuinely have the experience of seeing each hierophany in the framework of the symbolism it implied, and did always really *see* that symbolic system in every fragment which went to make it up.'[20] He refers to the source of these symbolic systems as the 'transconscious'.[21] However, it is not clear whether this, like Jung's collective unconscious, stores the symbolic systems, or whether, like Otto's faculty of divination, it is merely a potential for experiencing them.

In *The Sacred and the Profane*, published in 1957, Eliade discusses his concept of the sacred in greater detail, comparing it to a more theologically neutral version of Otto's concept of the numinous. Like Otto his interest is in describing the human experience of the divine, but in terms of both its apprehensible and mysterious aspects. As a result Eliade regards experience of the sacred as having a broader effect than experience of the numinous. As he puts it, experience of the sacred induces not only feelings but a mode of being, with the sacred and profane representing 'two modalities of experience ... two modes of being in the world'.[22] For Eliade, like Jung, sacred experience predominates in oral societies: 'The man of the archaic societies tends to live as much as possible *in* the sacred or in close proximity to consecrated objects.'[23] In contrast 'modern man has desacralised his world'.[24] For Eliade, again like Jung, this desacralisation, often now referred to as secularisation, is harmful because experience of the sacred resolves critical situations in that such experience contains a 'paradigmatic solution for every existential crisis'.[25]

Smart

·

Phenomenology continues to influence current developments in the study of the sacred, for example the work of Ninian Smart, formerly professor of religious studies at Lancaster University where he founded Britain's first major religious studies department. Smart is now professor of comparative religions at the University of California in the United States and his various publications include *Dimensions of the Sacred*, a study of the world's major living religions published in 1996.

In *Dimensions of the Sacred* Smart's emphasis is less on phenomenology as an approach to religious consciousness and more on its requirement of neutral description. As he puts it:

> In describing the way people behave, we do not use, so far as we can avoid them, alien categories to evoke the nature of their acts and to understand those acts. In this sense phenomenology is that attitude of informed empathy. It tries to bring out what religious acts mean to the actors.[26]

This change in emphasis enables Smart to provide an analysis of religion that is broader than that encompassed by earlier phenomenological studies. He argues that this wider range is important because an accurate description of religion requires the study of its various aspects, or dimensions as he refers to them. These dimensions are emotional, ritual, doctrinal, ethical, institutional, political, mythic or narrative, and material, that is the artistic expressions of religion from divine statues to cathedrals.

According to Smart such dimensional analysis has various advantages. It avoids imbalance in describing specific religions, for example ensuring that Hinduism is not discussed solely in terms of its mythic dimension, or Christianity only in terms of its doctrinal and ethical dimensions. And it enables change to be discussed in terms of interaction between different dimensions, avoiding the type of static description of a religion that Smart associates with an emphasis on one particular dimension. In addition, he suggests that dimensional analysis avoids the problem of defining religion, providing 'a kind of functional delineation of religions in lieu of a strict definition'.[27]

One of the particular difficulties Smart identifies in defining religion relates to the intellectualist argument that religion requires a belief in spiritual beings. Smart regards such a definition as inadequate: 'I am not saying that religion involves some belief, such as belief in God or gods, because in some religions, notably in Theravada Buddhism and Jainism and in phases of the Confucian tradition, such beliefs are secondary, to say the least.'[28] He also expresses doubts about the intellectualists' description of magic:

Older discussions reflected a lot about the societies which formulated the questions. For Victorians the issue of the distinction between religion and magic was important. This reflected varying strands in late Victorian values: the triumphant virtue of science; the spiritual superiority of Protestantism (and to some degree respectable Catholicism); the degeneracy of savages, etc.[29]

Because these Victorian values have given the term magic negative connotations, Smart prefers the phrase mantra causation, with mantra being a Sanskrit-derived word for a sacred formula. Despite this change in terminology, Smart's conception of magic is similar to the intellectualists', mantra causation being described as a way of causing change in the world through the use of sacred formulae rather than through spiritual beings: 'It supposes not that the events influenced by the mantra are powered by a spirit but that natural objects may jump to our commands.'[30]

Smart refers to a similar distinction between magic and religion in a discussion of performative utterances, a concept derived from linguistic philosophy and also much used in recent anthropological interpretation of ritual. Performative sentences are utterances in which an action is 'performed' by virtue of having been spoken, for example the statement 'I apologise for my mistake' itself constitutes an apology. Similarly, to cite an example of more relevance to religion, the statement 'I confess that I am a sinner' is itself a confession. Smart argues that ritual generally combines performative uses of language with formalised actions or behaviour. Religious ritual includes worship and sacrifice, and 'has as one of its major forms what may be called focused ritual, in which the ritual activity is addressed to sacred beings, such as gods or ancestors'.[31] In contrast 'methods analogous to religious ritual which are used to control forces in the world on behalf of human goals are typically referred to as magic'.[32]

Notes

•

1. Otto 1950: 12.
2. Otto 1950: 144.
3. Otto 1950: 132.
4. Otto 1950: 67.
5. Otto 1950: 118.
6. Otto 1950: 122.
7. Jung 1958a: 7.

 8. Jung 1958a: 7.
 9. Jung 1958a: 6.
10. Jung 1968b: 42.
11. Jung 1968b: 42.
12. Jung 1968b: 48.
13. Jung 1968a: 16.
14. Jung 1968a: 6.
15. Jung 1970a: 54.
16. Eliade 1979: 8.
17. Eliade 1979: 170.
18. Eliade 1979: 183.
19. Eliade 1979: 157–8.
20. Eliade 1979: 450.
21. Eliade 1979: 454.
22. Eliade 1959: 14.
23. Eliade 1959: 12.
24. Eliade 1959: 13.
25. Eliade 1959: 210.
26. Smart 1997: 2.
27. Smart 1997: 9.
28. Smart 1997: 9.
29. Smart 1997: 36.
30. Smart 1997: 109.
31. Smart 1997: 72.
32. Smart 1997: 72.

5

·

Structural-functional approaches

·

THE PREVIOUS CHAPTER DISCUSSED one of the principal approaches to the study of the sacred taken by historians of religion in the twentieth century. This chapter returns to the disciplines of anthropology and sociology, as well as to the beginning of the century, opening with a discussion of the work of the French sociologist Durkheim to which many subsequent structural-functional studies of the sacred have been indebted. The type of approach now referred to as structural functionalism has origins which can be traced back further than Durkheim's work, in particular to Spencer's argument that a society, like an organism, consists of specialised, mutually dependent parts, each functioning to maintain that society and meet its needs. Structural functionalism extends this argument, regarding religion not only as a specialised part within a society but also as having a structure which is determined by social structure. Structural functionalism therefore places much less emphasis on the individual than is the case in intellectualist and emotionalist approaches. In addition, its emphasis on social integration has led to charges that it ignores the questions of conflict and change within a society.

In addition to Durkheim, various other scholars – Mauss, Radcliffe-Brown and Evans-Pritchard – are discussed in this chapter. While Durkheim concentrated on religion, his colleague Mauss analysed the second aspect of the sacred, magic. Both these scholars had concerns beyond what is now referred to as structural functionalism. However, that particular aspect of their thought was especially influential on Radcliffe-Brown who in the late 1930s replaced Malinowski as the leading figure in British anthropology. Structural functionalism was not accepted unreservedly in British anthropology and the work of Radcliffe-Brown's successor Evans-Pritchard raises some questions about its merits. The chapter ends by summarising various recently proposed distinctions between magic and religion which relate to that made in structural functionalism.

Durkheim

Alongside Weber, Émile Durkheim (1858–1917) was the major figure in the early academic history of sociology. After studying philosophy in France and social theory in Germany, in 1887 he became the first ever lecturer in social studies at a French university, at Bordeaux. In 1892 he transferred to the Sorbonne, part of the University of Paris, where he taught for the rest of his life. During this period he established sociology as an academic discipline, accompanied by its own research journal, *Année Sociologique*, and in 1913 became Europe's first professor of sociology.

Durkheim regarded a society as much more than the sum of the individuals of which it is composed, viewing it as an entity that governs the mental processes and actions of its members, including their religious thought and behaviour. In addition he argued that a society's collective values, and the established patterns of social behaviour that accompany them, have a similar reality to the physical objects studied in the natural sciences. Such values and behaviour, social facts in his phrase, should therefore be studied in the same way as natural scientists study the physical world. As a result Durkheim discounted the role of the individual in his studies, arguing that most social facts precede individuals and that, even when individuals collaborate to create social facts, a gap exists between their intentions and what they create.

Durkheim's *The Elementary Forms of the Religious Life*, published in 1912, is generally regarded as the culmination of his academic work. He begins this book by using Buddhism as an example to dismiss the intellectualist argument that religion requires a belief in spiritual beings: 'Religion is more than the idea of gods or spirits, and consequently cannot be defined exclusively in relation to these latter.'[1] Instead he distinguishes between the sacred and the profane:

> All known religious beliefs, whether simple or complex, present one common characteristic: they presuppose a classification of all the things, real and ideal, of which men think, into two classes or opposed groups, gener-

ally designated by two distinct terms which are translated well enough by the words *profane* and *sacred*.[2]

It is in terms of the sacred that Durkheim begins his definition of religion: 'A religion is a unified system of beliefs and practices relative to sacred things, that is to say, things set apart and forbidden.'[3] He regards this statement as being equally applicable to magic. Thus his definition continues that religious beliefs and practices are socially integrating, that is they 'unite into one single moral community'.[4] In contrast, the belief in magic 'does not result in binding together those who adhere to it, nor in uniting them into a group leading a common life'.[5]

Later in *The Elementary Forms of the Religious Life* Durkheim proposes two further distinctions between magic and religion, one concerned with the nature of transgressions and the other with the nature of prohibitions. Firstly, he suggests that religious transgressions are punished on two levels, by misfortune and by condemnation: 'Even when the sacrilege has been punished, as it were, by the sickness or natural death of its author, it is also defamed; it offends opinion, which reacts against it; it puts the man who did it in fault.'[6] In contrast, magical transgressions lead to punishment on only one level, misfortune: 'In this case disobedience is not a fault; it creates no indignation. There is no sin in magic.'[7] Secondly, he suggests that while a religious prohibition implies the notion of sacredness, magical prohibitions imply 'a lay notion of property'.[8] Thus, when a magician requests that sacred things be avoided, 'it is not through respect for them and fear that they may be profaned ... it is merely for reasons of temporal utility'.[9] However, Durkheim accepts that such distinctions remain difficult to apply: 'This is not saying that there is a radical break of continuity between the religious and magic interdictions: on the contrary, it is one whose true nature is not decided.'[10]

In *The Elementary Forms of the Religious Life* Durkheim makes an assumption similar to one made by the intellectualists, that a society with the simplest technology will also have a religion of the most elementary kind. However, reflecting the difference between his definition of religion and that of the intellectualists, Durkheim argues that it is totemism, the worship not of deities but of animals and plants associated with particular social groups, that represents the most elementary form of religion. It is with an analysis of Australian totemism that his book is primarily concerned, with a view to providing a broader understanding of the nature of religion.

Durkheim argues that because a totem represents both a clan, to use his term, and what is religious to a clan, the clan is ultimately worshipping itself, with the totem symbolising the clan: 'If it [the totem] is at once the symbol of the god and of society, is that not because the god and the society are only one?'[11] As he continues: 'The god of the clan, the totemic principle, can ... be nothing else than the clan itself, personified and represented to the imagination under the visible form of the animal or vegetable which serves as totem.'[12]

But religion not only symbolises social structure, it is also a classificatory system, and in classifying the world it affects our perception of that world. For Durkheim classification begins with social structure: 'It is because men were organised that they have been able to organise things.'[13] Social classification therefore provides the basis for the religious classification of plants and animals in totemism: 'All known things will thus be arranged in a sort of tableau or systematic classification embracing the whole of nature.'[14] Religious classification subsequently provides a model for other classificatory systems such as science:

> Religion sets itself to translate ... realities into an intelligible language which does not differ from that employed by science; the attempt is made by both to connect things with each other, to establish internal relations between them, to classify them and to systematise them.[15]

Thus, as he puts it, 'the essential ideas of scientific logic are of religious origin'.[16]

According to Durkheim, religion has a third feature. In addition to symbolising social structure and serving as a classificatory system, it functions to integrate society by reaffirming social identity: 'Rites are means by which the social group reinforces itself periodically.'[17] More specifically, religious ritual contributes to the moral unity that Durkheim associates with society: 'Men who feel themselves united, partially by bonds of blood, but still more by a community of interest and tradition, assemble and become conscious of their moral unity.'[18]

Durkheim also discusses Frazer's principles of sympathetic magic, arguing that they are religious in origin: 'Magic forces have been conceived on the model of religious forces.'[19] Rather than homeopathic magic he therefore refers to imitative rites, and rather than contagious magic to the contagiousness of sacredness. He also defines contagiousness more broadly than Frazer, regarding it as a power of transfer: 'A condition or a good or bad quality is communicated contagiously from one subject to another who has some connection with the former.'[20]

Durkheim's analysis of imitative rites includes a discussion of fertility rituals featuring the marriage of vegetation deities. Such rituals are classified as magical by various scholars, for example by Frazer because they involve coercion of deities and by Malinowski because they have a practical aim of meeting a nutritional need. However, in Durkheim's terms they are religious because they function to integrate society, or more precisely because of their contribution to the moral unity of society: 'The true justification of religious practices does not lie in the apparent ends which they pursue, but rather in ... awakening or reawakening the sentiment of the moral comfort attained by the regular celebration of the cult.'[21]

Durkheim regards this implicit function of ritual as explaining why people believe in ritual's practical efficacy:

> So manifest an error seems hardly intelligible so long as we see in the rite only the material end towards which it seems to aim. But we know that in addition to the effect it is thought to have ... it also exercises a profound influence over the souls of the worshippers who take part in it.[22]

He argues similarly that 'the moral efficacy of the rite, which is real, leads to the belief in its physical efficacy, which is imaginary'.[23] For Durkheim, while rituals may be explicitly concerned with, for example, ensuring fertility, of more importance is this implicit function, 'the invisible action which they exercise over the mind'.[24] Thus, in his view, even though people believe that their ritual acts on things it is in fact their minds that are acted on.

Mauss

Marcel Mauss (1872–1950), Durkheim's nephew, trained originally as a philosopher at the Universities of Paris and Bordeaux before becoming a professional researcher in sociology, working for *Année Sociologique* from 1898, and then holding various academic posts from 1901 onwards. His wide range of publications includes *A General Theory of Magic*, published early in his career in 1902–3, in which he analyses that part of the sacred, magic, not treated by Durkheim. He broadly uses the same distinction between magic and religion but takes a more comparative approach by drawing examples of magic from various societies.

In *A General Theory of Magic* Mauss proposes a distinction between magic and religion which is similar to Durkheim's: 'A magical rite is *any rite which does not play a part in organised cults* – it is private, secret, mysterious and approaches the limit of a prohibited rite.'[25] In contrast, religious rites are those that do belong to organised cults. It follows from this definition that 'magical and religious rites often have different agents; in other words, they are not performed by one and the same person',[26] and that magical rituals do not generally take place 'inside a temple or at some domestic shrine'.[27] However, Mauss accepts that there are difficulties with this distinction in that, for example, rain-making, which he regards as magical, is not performed in secret but in public. His solution to this problem is to identify such rituals as essentially rather than wholly magical: 'One thing is certain, and that is that they are basic to magic.'[28]

In defining magic in this way, Mauss is able to challenge Frazer's distinctions between magic and religion. In relation to sympathetic magic he argues: 'There are not only magical rites which are not sympathetic, but neither is sympathy a prerogative of magic, since there are sympathetic practices in religion.'[29] Nor are spiritual agents absent from magic: 'Spirits and even gods may be involved in magic.'[30] Nor is magic solely coercive and religion solely propitiating: 'Religious rites may also constrain and ... spirits, gods and devils do not always automatically obey the orders of a magician; the latter is often forced to supplicate them.'[31]

More fundamentally, Mauss argues that the primary feature of magic is a belief in an impersonal power with 'automatic efficacy'.[32] It is this power that underlies secondary features such as sympathetic magic: 'Sympathy is the route along which magical powers pass: it does not provide magical power itself.'[33] This power also lies behind the magical properties, such as the yellowness of a root chosen to cure jaundice, that are transferred by sympathetic magic: 'Magical attributes are not conceived as being naturally, absolutely and specifically contained in the object to which they are attached; they are always relatively extrinsic and conferred.'[34]

However, this power also represents 'the rudimentary data of religion'.[35] From this it follows that religion and magic 'both derive from the same source',[36] in contrast to Frazer's proposal that religion developed from the failure of magic as an explanatory model. In fact, Mauss argues the opposite, suggesting that religion preceded magic because religion, being 'essentially a collective phenomenon',[37] developed from society, some of whose members subsequently 'merely appropriated to themselves the collective forces of society'.[38]

Mauss also discusses the relationship between magic and science, to a degree again differing with Frazer's view that magic and science are similar. Against Frazer he argues that there is a fundamental difference between magic and science because in magic 'it is not really believed that the gestures themselves bring about the results'.[39] Instead 'the effect derives from something else, and usually this is not of the same order'.[40] However, he suggests that there is an affinity between magic and science as classificatory systems, arguing that the magician's classifying of the concrete properties of magical objects is an activity for which 'we are willing to accord him the title of scientist'.[41] Similarly, because of the emphasis in magic on classification of the concrete it 'became an early store of information for the astronomical, physical and natural sciences'.[42]

Radcliffe-Brown

To a great degree the school of French sociology established by Durkheim was brought to an end by the First World War which started in 1914. However, Durkheim's approach was taken up in England, in particular by A. R. Radcliffe-Brown (1881–1955), a contemporary of Malinowski who in the late 1930s replaced him as the leading figure in British anthropology. Radcliffe-Brown studied anthropology at Cambridge University. Having held foundation chairs in the discipline at the Universities of Cape Town and Sydney, in 1937 he took the first established chair in anthropology at Oxford University. He left Oxford in 1946 and subsequently taught at the University of Chicago and elsewhere.

Radcliffe-Brown followed Malinowski in abandoning the British tradition of armchair scholarship represented by the intellectualists. However, he rejected Malinowski's social-psychological approach which emphasises the role society plays in meeting an individual's needs, favouring instead the social-structural aspects of Durkheim's work, emphasising a correspondence between a society's structure and its religion. Radcliffe-Brown did not publish a large body of work and the following discussion concentrates on two lectures he delivered in which he examined the nature of magic and religion in relation to the theories of Frazer, Malinowski and Durkheim.

In a lecture delivered in 1945 Radcliffe-Brown endorsed Durkheim's argument that religious structure is determined by social structure, describing how 'religion must also vary in correspondence with the manner in which the society is constituted'.[43] And, again like

Durkheim, he also argued that religion functions to integrate and maintain a society, describing how religious rituals 'regulate, maintain and transmit from one generation to another sentiments on which the constitution of the society depends'.[44]

As with Durkheim this approach leads to an emphasis on the implicit or symbolic functions of ritual, discussed by Radcliffe-Brown in a lecture delivered in 1939: 'The very common tendency to look for the explanation of ritual actions in their purpose is the result of a false assimilation of them to what may be called technical acts.'[45] He suggested instead that 'ritual acts differ from technical acts in having in all instances some expressive or symbolic element in them'.[46] This symbolic element, according to Radcliffe-Brown, operates in two ways, both structuring the ideas of a society and integrating that society.

In the same lecture Radcliffe-Brown contested Malinowski's emotionalist interpretation of magic and religion as providing relief and reassurance in times of stress:

> While one anthropological theory is that magic and religion give men confidence, comfort and a sense of security, it could equally well be argued that they give men fears and anxieties of which they would otherwise be free – the fear of black magic or of spirits, fear of God, of the Devil, of Hell.[47]

Radcliffe-Brown also discussed the various attempts made by Frazer, Malinowski and Durkheim to distinguish magic from religion, arguing that the distinctions were contradictory and that, though theoretically interesting, they were difficult to apply. Instead he suggested that 'a simple dichotomy between magic and religion'[48] was unhelpful, and that it was better to subsume both within the category of ritual, advice followed by many subsequent anthropologists.

Evans-Pritchard

While E. E. Evans-Pritchard (1902–73) studied under Radcliffe-Brown and in 1946 succeeded him as professor of anthropology at Oxford University, a post he held until his retirement in 1970, his work provides a much cooler endorsement of structural-functional theories. His discussions of magic and religion are primarily related to their occurrence in certain African oral societies. Reflecting this concern with the specific circumstances in which magic and religion occur, his approach is sometimes referred to as contextualist. More generally, however, his work combines an interest in the theoretical aspects of anthropology with the type of interpretive approach favoured by Weber and more frequently found in humanities disciplines such as history.

Evans-Pritchard's principal study of magic in a specific society is *Witchcraft, Oracles and Magic among the Azande* which was published in 1937. In this book he makes a distinction between two modes of thought similar in some ways to the distinction made by Radcliffe-Brown between symbolic and technical. Evans-Pritchard describes one mode of thought as mystical and the other as empirical, that is as based on observation and experiment. The mystical mode of thought, which in the case of the Azande involves witchcraft, oracles and magic, is defined as follows: 'These are patterns of thought that attribute to phenomena supra-sensible qualities which, or part of which, are not derived from observation or cannot be logically inferred from it, and which they do not possess.'[49]

Magic is Evans-Pritchard's translation of a Zande term and is a technique that is thought to achieve its purpose by the use of medicines: 'The operation of these medicines is a magic rite and is usually accompanied by a spell.'[50] These rituals are performed privately and thus conform with Mauss's definition of magic: 'All Zande ritual acts, even addresses to the ghost, are performed with a minimum of publicity. Good magic and bad magic alike are secretly enacted.'[51]

Evans-Pritchard regards the two modes of thought – mystical and empirical – as consistent in the context of the Zande system of beliefs. Thus, rather than contradicting empirical causation, Zande mystical thought supplements it by explaining why certain people suffer misfortune. As an example Evans-Pritchard discusses a granary eaten away by termites and collapsing on people sitting in it. The cause of the collapse is empirically understood to have been the termites. But this explanation is supplemented by the mystical concept of witchcraft which is used to account for the presence of the specific people there at the time of the collapse. As Evans-Pritchard puts it: 'The facts do not explain themselves or only partly explain themselves. They can only be explained fully if one takes witchcraft into consideration.'[52] The two other aspects of the mystical mode of thought – magic and oracles – are also consistent with this system of beliefs. Magic provides protection from witchcraft or a remedy to it, while oracles determine who is responsible for witchcraft or who faces it. As Evans-Pritchard puts it: 'Witchcraft, oracles and magic are like three sides to a triangle. Oracles and magic are two different ways of combating witchcraft.'[53]

A different African people, the Nuer, are the focus of Evans-Pritchard's major study of religion, *Nuer Religion* which was published in 1956. In this book he adopts the intellectualist definition of religion as requiring a belief in spiritual beings, but modifies it to accept as religious both coercion and propitiation of the spiritual beings. More specifically, religion among the Nuer involves a belief in one transcendental Spirit known as *kwoth*. In the context of this people's beliefs Evans-Pritchard regards magic as a supra-sensible quality which is unrelated to *kwoth*. Thus he refers to 'magical substances which have an efficacy in themselves and do not derive their power from Spirit'.[54] In contrast, he regards as religious any supra-sensible quality which is related to *kwoth*. Thus totems – *kwoth* in a material form – and the rituals associated with them are religious:

> We have observed that a totemic spirit sometimes gives a man certain powers over the totemic species. The rites these people perform might be classed, according to some definition of the term, as magic, but in the Nuer classification, which is the one we have to follow if we are to delineate their thought and not our own, we are still concerned with a relationship between man and *kwoth*.[55]

This interpretation of totemism thus opposes Malinowski's classification of it as magical. Evans-Pritchard also contests Malinowski's social-psychological view that totemism is society's method of responding to a basic human need, in this case a nutritional one: 'The facts of Nuer totemism do not, therefore, support the contention of those who see in totemism chiefly, or even merely, a ritualisation of empirical interests.'[56] Instead Evans-Pritchard takes a social-structural approach, relating 'the configuration of Nuer religious thought to the structural order of society'.[57] However, he thinks this approach shows only how social structure has influenced religious representation and reveals little about the nature of *kwoth*: 'A structural interpretation explains only certain characteristics of the refractions and not the idea of Spirit in itself.'[58] He therefore expresses doubts about the structural-functional approach:

> Durkheim and his colleagues and pupils were not content to say that religion, being part of the social life, is strongly influenced by the social structure. They claimed that the religious conceptions of primitive peoples are nothing more than a symbolic representation of the social order.[59]

Evans-Pritchard also contests interpretations of sacrifice that regard it as a form of union with the divine, suggesting that it is often concerned with avoiding harmful divine intervention rather than attracting its helpful equivalent. For example, he argues that among the Nuer private sacrifice is primarily designed to counter divinely caused misfortune: 'The purpose of Nuer piacular [expiatory] sacrifices is to establish communication with God rather in order to keep him away or get rid of him than to establish a union or fellowship with him.'[60] For the Nuer, such misfortune is explained in terms of transgression, as opposed to the Azande who explain it in terms of witchcraft: 'Nuer think that a man would not be sick if there had been no error.'[61] Consequently Nuer cures for illness are religious rather than the magical medicines of the Azande: 'Since sickness is the action of Spirit therapeutic treatment is sacramental.'[62]

Related distinctions between religion and magic

The central distinction proposed between religion and magic by Durkheim, that religion is collective and socially integrating while magic is more individualist, has been developed in various ways by later scholars less influenced by the social-structural aspects of his thoughts. One example of such a development is provided by an article by Mischa Titiev which was published in 1960. Titiev begins this article by arguing that magic and religion are both methods 'for trying to gain desired ends',[63] and that both 'appeal to the supernatural world for help, guidance or comfort'.[64]

To distinguish between the two he proposes a modified version of Durkheim's distinction, suggesting that religious ritual appeals to the supernatural on a calendrical, collective basis while magic does so on a critical, individualist basis. He defines calendrical ritual as recurrent, scheduled, generally performed by priests and 'social or communal in character'.[65] In contrast, critical rituals are irregular, unscheduled and generally not performed by priests. While they can be performed to benefit society, 'for the most part critical ceremonies are staged only when a private or personal emergency has arisen'.[66]

While Titiev was concerned with the broad question of distinguishing magic from religion, other scholars have examined historical usages of the term magic. For example, the negative connotations that magic had in the Greco-Roman world are discussed by Jonathan Z. Smith in an article published in 1975. Smith supports Durkheim's emphasis on a social distinction between magic and religion: 'One of the more important insights was brought forth by the French Sociological School which argued that magic was not different in essence from religion, but rather different with respect to social position.'[67] Reflecting its lower social position, magic was used in the Greco-Roman world as a term of condemnation, so that, for example, writers hostile to Christianity accused Christ of having been a magician. During this period magic, described by Mauss as approaching the limit of a prohibited rite, crossed the borderline into illegality. As Smith puts it, in this period there is 'one, universal characteristic of magic – it is illegal; within the Greco-Roman world it carried the penalty of death or deportation'.[68]

Notes

1. Durkheim 1976: 35.
2. Durkheim 1976: 37.
3. Durkheim 1976: 47.
4. Durkheim 1976: 47.
5. Durkheim 1976: 44.
6. Durkheim 1976: 300.
7. Durkheim 1976: 301.
8. Durkheim 1976: 301.
9. Durkheim 1976: 301.
10. Durkheim 1976: 301 note 2.
11. Durkheim 1976: 206.
12. Durkheim 1976: 206.
13. Durkheim 1976: 145.
14. Durkheim 1976: 142.
15. Durkheim 1976: 429.
16. Durkheim 1976: 429.
17. Durkheim 1976: 387.
18. Durkheim 1976: 387.
19. Durkheim 1976: 324 note 1.
20. Durkheim 1976: 356.
21. Durkheim 1976: 360.
22. Durkheim 1976: 359.
23. Durkheim 1976: 359.
24. Durkheim 1976: 360.
25. Mauss 1972: 24.
26. Mauss 1972: 23.
27. Mauss 1972: 23.
28. Mauss 1972: 135.
29. Mauss 1972: 20–1.

30. Mauss 1972: 21.
31. Mauss 1972: 21.
32. Mauss 1972: 117.
33. Mauss 1972: 102.
34. Mauss 1972: 102.
35. Mauss 1972: 137.
36. Mauss 1972: 137.
37. Mauss 1972: 90.
38. Mauss 1972: 90.
39. Mauss 1972: 20.
40. Mauss 1972: 20.
41. Mauss 1972: 76.
42. Mauss 1972: 143.
43. Radcliffe-Brown 1956b: 161.
44. Radcliffe-Brown 1956b: 157.
45. Radcliffe-Brown 1956a: 143.
46. Radcliffe-Brown 1956a: 143.
47. Radcliffe-Brown 1956a: 149.
48. Radcliffe-Brown 1956a: 138.
49. Evans-Pritchard 1937: 12.
50. Evans-Pritchard 1937: 9.
51. Evans-Pritchard 1937: 424.
52. Evans-Pritchard 1937: 71.
53. Evans-Pritchard 1937: 387.
54. Evans-Pritchard 1956: 104.
55. Evans-Pritchard 1956: 95.
56. Evans-Pritchard 1956: 80.
57. Evans-Pritchard 1956: 119.
58. Evans-Pritchard 1956: 121.
59. Evans-Pritchard 1956: 313.
60. Evans-Pritchard 1956: 275.
61. Evans-Pritchard 1956: 192.
62. Evans-Pritchard 1956: 192.
63. Titiev 1965: 319.
64. Titiev 1965: 317.
65. Titiev 1965: 317.
66. Titiev 1965: 318.
67. Smith 1978a: 192.
68. Smith 1978a: 192.

6
.
Symbolic approaches
.

D ESPITE EVANS-PRITCHARD'S RESERVATIONS, structural functionalism has influenced many anthropological studies of religion
written since the end of the Second World War. As discussed in the
previous chapter, structural functionalism regards religion as a particular type of symbolic system: in a narrow sense religion symbolises
social structure, but in a broader sense it is a symbolic means of
expressing collective values. Such interpretations of religion stress this
type of implicit function rather than any explicit function such as, for
example, appealing to deities for a good harvest.

This opposition between implicit and explicit is often expressed in
other ways, in particular in terms of symbolist versus literalist. Symbolist
approaches to religion are represented in this chapter by the work of two
post-war British anthropologists, Douglas and Beattie, while literalist
approaches, associated with a revival of the intellectualist interpretation
of religion, are discussed in the next chapter. Douglas and Beattie were
particularly indebted to Durkheim, but Douglas was also influenced by
two other Continental scholars from the beginning of the twentieth century, Lévy-Bruhl and van Gennep, both contemporaries of Durkheim,
and it is with summaries of those scholars' work that this chapter begins.

Symbolist approaches represent only one of many interpretations
of religion and magic as symbolic. Various other interpretations have
already been discussed, most of which regard such symbolism as
being deliberately intended or as something of which ritual participants are aware. For example, the early intellectualists related magic
to the performance of actions symbolising a desired event, as in the
case of sacred marriages symbolising agricultural fertility. Weber also
regarded such practices as symbolic, but argued in addition that the

perception of any event as being divinely influenced is symbolic, with the natural world being regarded as containing symbols of the supernatural world. Eliade referred more specifically to symbolic systems which he discussed as lying behind various manifestations of the sacred in nature. In these terms religion symbolises something about the supernatural order, in contrast to symbolist approaches which emphasise what religion symbolises about the social order. Returning to the area of implicit symbolism favoured by the symbolists, but offering a very different interpretation of religion, Freud argued that religion symbolises repressed Oedipal feelings towards one's father.

Various further interpretations of religion and magic as symbolic are discussed in this chapter in relation to the work of the post-war anthropologists Turner, Tambiah and Geertz. Turner's particular emphasis is on ritual, which he regards as featuring items symbolising basic biological and psychological processes, while Tambiah's emphasis is on magic whose symbolism he relates to particular rhetorical techniques. The chapter ends by discussing the distinctive contribution of the American anthropologist Geertz, who regards religion as symbolising cosmic frameworks of order and argues, against the structural functionalists, that religion is better viewed as shaping social structure than as being shaped by it, an argument reminiscent of Weber's discussion of the influence of Protestantism on the rise of capitalism.

Lévy-Bruhl

Lucien Lévy-Bruhl (1857–1939) began his academic career as a philosopher and in 1904 was appointed to a chair in the history of modern philosophy at the Sorbonne. Much of his work was dedicated to the subject of what he referred to as primitive mentality as distinct from Western logic. Later scholars have generally rejected the distinctions he proposed between these two modes of thought, although Jung was particularly influenced by his concept of primitive mentality. However, a contrast between two modes of thought, such as Radcliffe-Brown's between expressive and technical and Evans-Pritchard's between mystical and empirical, is a feature of many subsequent discussions of magic and religion as symbolic. Such discussions have also tended to follow Lévy-Bruhl in subsuming magic and religion within whatever category – symbolic, expressive, mystical – is substituted for his primitive mentality.

In his research into primitive mentality Lévy-Bruhl, like many other scholars in this period, relied on a wide range of secondary sources describing oral societies. Also like many of his contemporaries, in particular the intellectualists, he was interested in the question of the evolution of society. Unlike the intellectualists, however, he related this evolution to different modes of thought and envisaged it as consisting broadly of only two stages, primitive mentality followed by Western logic. More precisely he related social evolution to different sociomental processes, rejecting the intellectualist emphasis on the individual and favouring Durkheim's emphasis on the social or collective.

Lévy-Bruhl's theories are set forth in *How Natives Think*, published in 1910, although it should be mentioned that in his later years he modified his views, regarding the two modes of thought as co-existing rather than sequential and moderating the contrast between the two. Lévy-Bruhl begins *How Natives Think* by arguing that intellectualist interpretations of magic and religion 'deal with the mental processes of *the individual human mind* only'[1] and that they are therefore inappropriate to collective phenomena such as magic and religion. He also suggests that it is inappropriate to think that primitive thought corresponds to that of the intellectualists: 'They take it for granted that the ways which, to our minds, seem to lead naturally to certain beliefs and practices are precisely those trodden by the members of the communities in which they are found.'[2]

He thinks this assumption is incorrect because it fails to recognise that different types of society have different modes of thought: 'A definite type of society, with its own institutions and customs, will ... have its own mentality.'[3] He focuses on one particular type of society, referred to as primitive, and suggests that its mode of thought, instead of being a poorer version of our own, as the intellectualists argue, is a different way of thinking based on a logic other than ours.

He characterises primitive thought as mystic 'in the strictly defined sense in which "mystic" implies belief in forces and influences and actions which, though imperceptible to sense, are nevertheless real'.[4] In primitive thought 'everything that exists possesses mystic properties'[5] and consequently 'primitives perceive nothing in the same way as we do'.[6] Both objective and subjective reality are perceived mystically, so the distinction does not exist in primitive thought: 'This accounts for the confidence which the primitive has in his dreams, a confidence which is at least as great as that he accords his ordinary perceptions.'[7] Nor is there any distinction between the natural and the supernatural: 'The primitive's mentality does not recognise two distinct worlds in contact with each other, and more or less interpenetrating. To him there is but one. Every reality, like every influence, is mystic, and consequently every perception is also mystic.'[8]

According to Lévy-Bruhl, spatial and temporal connections in primitive thought are also conceived mystically, by what he refers to as the law of participation, described as 'a mystic influence which is communicated, under conditions themselves of mystic nature, from one being or object to another'.[9] Lévy-Bruhl concludes by briefly examining the transition from primitive to Western thought, describing the latter as a logic that seeks to identify contradictions and 'which tends to realise itself through the purely conceptual and the intellectual treatment of pure concepts'.[10]

Van Gennep

Arnold van Gennep (1873–1957), who was born in Germany and educated mostly in France, was a prolific gatherer of folklore from European and other societies. He worked broadly within the tradition of Frazer, whose *The Golden Bough* he translated into French. For much of his life this approach made him an academic outsider because of the dominance of the Durkheim school in France, although he became a professor in Switzerland, at the University of Neuchâtel. While his work as a compiler of folklore was in some ways similar to Frazer's, he was more analytical than Frazer, and it is for his analysis of the structure and symbolism of a certain type of ritual, referred to as rites of passage, that he is now best known in anthropology.

In *The Rites of Passage*, published in 1908, van Gennep is primarily concerned with ritual marking the individual's life cycle and involving a passage from one condition to another, such as ritual relating to birth, marriage and death. His analysis, based on examples of such ritual drawn from various societies, places particular emphasis on rites of social transition that enable a passage from one social status or occupation to another. However, subsequent scholars have expanded his analysis to apply to most forms of ritual.

Van Gennep begins *The Rites of Passage* by addressing the question of distinguishing magic from religion, arguing that the two co-exist and that religion is a kind of theoretical adjunct to a wide range of techniques, all of which he regards as magical. He distinguishes between two broad types of religious theory: dynamism, such as Marett's pre-animism, in which supernatural power is impersonal; and animism, a category broader than Tylor's, in which supernatural power has the attributes of a conscious being. He divides magic into three different types of technique: Frazer's sympathetic magic; spoken magic, direct such as spells and indirect such as prayers; and injunctions, both positive and negative, with the latter including taboos. As he puts it: 'These theories constitute *religion*, whose techniques (ceremonies, rites, services) I call *magic*.'[11]

Van Gennep analyses rites of passage as having a common structure consisting of three stages: separation, transition and incorporation. He thinks this three-stage structure is most clearly shown in initiation ritual in which the individual is first removed from society in a separation ritual, transformed in a transition ritual, and then returned to society with a new social status in an incorporation ritual. He interprets many ritual activities as symbolising one of these three stages. Thus, for example, circumcision symbolises separation, exchange of gifts symbolises transition, and a shared meal symbolises incorporation. Similarly, fertility rituals are interpreted as rites of passage in which the death of vegetation deities symbolises separation, their absence symbolises transition and their resurrection symbolises integration.

Van Gennep's analysis has been particularly influential in two respects. One is in the general area of bodily symbolism, that is in discussion of the human body as an object that can be marked to convey symbolic information, as in his interpretation of circumcision as symbolising separation. The other is in the importance attached to the transformative power of the transition stage in rites of passage. This power is now often referred to as liminality, from *limen*, the Latin word for threshold, indicating the status of the transition stage as outside the normal constraints of human time and space, and as having access to a different set of conditions that are both more powerful and more dangerous.

Douglas

The wide-ranging work of Mary Douglas, a student and subsequently colleague of Evans-Pritchard, includes studies resulting from fieldwork among African oral societies as well as more comparative publications examining the relationship between social structure and religion and magic. The following discussion concentrates on two of these comparative studies, *Purity and Danger*, published in 1966, and *Natural Symbols*, published in 1970. Both reveal the influence of Durkheim and van Gennep while the first also acknowledges the influence of Lévy-Bruhl, an approach which is rejected in the second.

Purity and Danger is primarily a study of concepts of pollution, meaning in this context objects and persons regarded both as impure and as capable of transferring that impurity contagiously to others, that is as being both polluted and polluting. Douglas begins by comparing concepts of pollution to the Western attitude to dirt. As she puts it: 'Dirt offends against order. Eliminating it is not a negative movement, but a positive effort to organise the environment.'[12] The various responses to pollution, such as purification or prohibiting its bearers, similarly order the environment: 'Ideas about separating, purifying, demarcating and punishing transgressions have as their main function to impose system on an inherently untidy experience.'[13]

Following Durkheim, she also suggests that many concepts of pollution 'are used as analogies for expressing a general view of the social order'.[14] And, following van Gennep, she adds that these analogies can be expressed in terms of bodily symbolism, with the body being used as a symbolic medium to express a particular social structure. Thus, for example, 'bodily perfection can symbolise an ideal theocracy [a society governed by a deity or priesthood]'.[15] Before discussing these ideas in more detail, Douglas considers the distinctions made between magic and religion by Durkheim on the one hand and by Tylor and Frazer on the other.

She regards Tylor and Frazer's distinction between magic as automatically efficacious and religion as more variably so, as an ill-considered version of a 'sectarian quarrel about the value of formal ritual'.[16] Frazer in particular is attacked for converting this quarrel into an evolutionary scheme in which magic precedes religion: 'This fashionable presentation was supported by no evidence whatever.'[17] Later Douglas also attacks Malinowski for interpreting magic as a kind of support-system in times of stress: 'How could he have barrenly isolated magic rite from other rites and discussed magic as a kind of poor man's whisky, used for gaining conviviality and courage against daunting odds?'[18]

The intellectualist argument that magic and religion represent explanatory models is also discussed. Douglas suggests that magic and religion are not so much designed to explain events in nature as to organise society: 'Questions are not phrased primarily to satisfy man's curiosity about the seasons and the rest of the natural environment. They are phrased to satisfy a dominant social concern, the problem of how to organise together in society.'[19] However, she agrees that religion and magic are to an extent explanatory, focusing on the concepts they use to account for misfortune, which she refers to as cosmologies, and again relating them to social issues:

If social life in a particular community has settled down into any sort of constant form, social problems tend to crop up in the same areas of tension or strife. And so as part of the machinery for resolving them, these beliefs about automatic punishment, destiny, ghostly vengeance and witchcraft crystallise in the institutions.[20]

Durkheim too is attacked by Douglas for the terms in which he distinguished magic from religion. She endorses his social-structural approach to religion for recognising 'that primitive gods are part and parcel of the community, their form expressing accurately the details of its structure'.[21] However, she rejects his distinction between religion as integrating and magic as not. She argues that the two should not be separated because both symbolise social structure and feature similar concepts of contagion: 'Durkheim's idea of ritual as symbolic of social processes can be extended to include both types of belief in contagion, religious and magical.'[22] Douglas therefore praises Radcliffe-Brown for incorporating magic and religion within ritual but argues that his approach has resulted in sacred and secular ritual being separated. She thinks instead that the two are continuous, as exemplified by her analogy between concepts of pollution and Western attitudes to dirt.

Douglas also discusses Lévy-Bruhl's contrast between two modes of thought: primitive thought and Western logic. Rather than Western logic being more concerned with identifying contradictions, she suggests that, just as Western society is more differentiated, so too is its mode of thought: 'Our experiences take place in separate compartments and our rituals too.'[23] She argues similarly that 'we moderns operate in many different fields of symbolic action'.[24] In contrast the mode of thought in oral societies is undifferentiated: 'All their contexts of experience overlap and interpenetrate, nearly all their experience is religious.'[25] Consequently 'their rituals create one single, symbolically consistent universe'.[26]

In her discussion of pollution, Douglas's broad argument is that the specification of particular items as impure or as prohibited constitutes a classificatory system which orders the environment. Her discussion focuses on different sets of dietary prohibitions involving animals, primarily prohibitions recorded in the Old Testament and ones observed by African oral societies. She argues that these prohibitions classify the animal kingdom and show a correspondence between the animal, cosmological and social categories: 'So far from being meaningless, it is primitive magic which gives meaning to existence. This applies as much to the negative as to the positive rites. The prohibitions trace the cosmic outlines and the ideal social order.'[27] Such rituals therefore have both an implicit function of providing meaning and order as well as an explicitly instrumental function: 'Instrumental efficacy is not the only kind of efficacy to be derived from their symbolic action. The other kind is achieved in the action itself, in the assertions it makes and the experience which bears its imprinting.'[28]

Douglas draws particular attention to what she refers to as anomalous animals, that is animals that transgress or cannot be placed within such systems of classification: 'Those whose behaviour is ambiguous are treated as anomalies of one kind or another and are struck off someone's diet sheet.'[29] She argues that in addition to being prohibited, an anomalous animal, because it resists classification, 'symbolises both danger and power'.[30] Douglas extends this argument to apply to the transition stage in van Gennep's tripartite analysis of rites of passage, suggesting that danger attaches to any situation outside the dominant system of classification: 'Danger lies in transitional states; simply because transition is neither one state nor the next, it is undefinable. The person who must pass from one to another is himself in danger and emanates danger to others.'[31]

In addition to dietary prohibitions, Douglas discusses other concepts of pollution, in particular those associated with the body, arguing that concern for the bodily margins reflects concern about society:

> We cannot possibly interpret rituals concerning excreta, breast milk, saliva and the rest unless we are prepared to see in the body a symbol of society, and to see the powers and dangers credited to social structure reproduced in small on the human body.[32]

Thus there is a correspondence between bodily pollutions and the body politic: 'When rituals express anxiety about the body's orifices, the sociological counterpart of this anxiety is a care to protect the political and cultural continuity of a cultural group.'[33] As Douglas puts it: 'The body ... provides a basic scheme for all symbolism. There is hardly any pollution which does not have some primary physiological reference.'[34]

In *Natural Symbols* Douglas continues her interest in the relationship between symbolic systems and social structure: 'We will look for tendencies and correlations between the character of the symbolic system and that of the social system.'[35] Again, too, bodily symbolism is related to social structure: 'The organic system provides an analogy of the social system.'[36] However, she abandons the distinction made in *Purity and Danger* between two contrasting modes of thought. Instead, one of the principal concerns of *Natural Symbols* is establishing a correlation between different types of social influence and different types of symbolism.

Before discussing these types of social influence, Douglas returns to the problem of distinguishing between magic and religion, favouring instead a distinction between low and high ritualism, with ritualism being defined as 'a concern that efficacious symbols be correctly manipulated and that the right words be pronounced in the right order'.[37] This broad distinction aligns the low ritualism of ascetic Protestantism with the Nuer religion discussed by Evans-Pritchard, and the high ritualism of traditional Catholicism with Bantu magic. As Douglas puts it: 'I see no advantage for this discussion in making any distinction between magical and sacramental.'[38]

Having distinguished between these two attitudes towards ritual, Douglas goes on to discuss two dimensions of social influence: in one dimension, grid, the individual is influenced by society-wide forces, 'order, classification, the symbolic system',[39] while in the other dimension, group, the individual is influenced by social relationships. Both dimensions range from strong to weak: hermits provide an example of weak group and communes of strong; weak grid is characterised by high individual autonomy and strong by low individual autonomy. Douglas regards different societies, or parts of a society, as having different combinations of these dimensions, for example combining strong group with weak grid or being strong in both. According to Douglas, the same combination of grid and group is likely to have, among other characteristics, the same attitude to ritual, the same bodily symbolism and the same type of cosmology, with cosmology again being used to refer to concepts of what causes good and bad fortune.

For example, where both dimensions are strong, high ritualism is expected along with a cosmology that rewards good and punishes evil: 'Strong grid and strong group will tend to a routinised piety towards authority and its symbols; beliefs in a punishing, moral universe; and a category of rejects.'[40] In contrast, where the group dimension is strong and the grid weak cosmology is likely to be dualist, with good and evil being regarded as vying for control of the cosmos. Douglas suggests that witchcraft-belief represents one example of such a dualist cosmology: 'Its doctrine of two kinds of humanity, one good, the other bad, and the association of the badness of some humans with cosmic powers of evil is basically similar to some of the so-called dualist religions.'[41]

Later Douglas discusses the particular types of bodily symbolism associated with these two combinations of grid and group. For the first she suggests:

> The religious emphasis would be expected to treat the body as the focus and symbol of life. We would expect to find positive themes of symbolic nourishment developed to the extent that the social body and the physical body are assimilated and both focus the identity of individuals in a structured, bounded system.[42]

For the second: 'We would expect to find the body an object of anxiety; fear of poisoning and debilitation would be dominant and ritual officiants much concerned with therapy, physical and social.'[43]

Elsewhere, in an article published in 1968, Douglas offers a social-structural interpretation of rites of social transition: 'Rites of passage ... define entrance to a new status. In this way the permanence and value of the classifications embracing all sections of society are emphasised.'[44] Van Gennep's own discussion of the function of such rites is more social-psychological and provides some indication of the difference in emphasis between the two types of approach: 'Such changes of condition do not occur without disturbing the life of society and the individual, and it is the function of rites of passage to reduce their harmful effects.'[45]

Beattie

In an article published in 1970 and directed against the intellectualist revival discussed in the following chapter, the British anthropologist J. H. M. Beattie interprets religious symbolism in a manner similar to Douglas. In this article Beattie also returns to the question of two co-exisiting and contrasting modes of thought, distinguishing between symbolic and scientific, variations on the earlier distinctions made by Radcliffe-Brown between expressive and technical and by Evans-Pritchard between mystical and empirical.

Beattie describes magico-religious symbols as representing 'some more or less abstract notion (power, social or group unity, "maleness" and "femaleness", life, the dangerous and unfamiliar, are examples) to which social or cultural value, either positive or negative, is attached'.[46] He associates this type of symbolic thought not only with magic and religion but also with art, and contrasts it with scientific thought. He regards this contrast as, to varying degrees, being denied by intellectualist approaches which emphasise only one, progressively improving mode of thought.

Thus, for example, Beattie attacks Frazer for describing magic as a poor science and ignoring its symbolic aspect: 'The savage ... knew better than Frazer did ... that when he was making magic he was performing a rite, not applying laws of nature, however dimly apprehended.'[47] For Beattie ritual involves a combination of practical and symbolic action. The former can be understood 'when the ends sought and the techniques used by the actor are grasped'.[48] The latter, however, cannot be understood in this way; instead its understanding requires 'comprehension of the meanings which the participant's ideas and acts have, or may have, as symbolic statements'.[49]

Turner

Much of the early work of the British anthropologist Victor Turner can be viewed as being influenced by the social-psychological tradition, including many aspects of his interpretation of ritual symbolism on which the following discussion concentrates. Also discussed is some of his later work in which the influence of van Gennep is apparent.

In *Schism and Continuity in an African Society*, published in 1957, Turner examines the relationship between ritual and social structure, focusing on Ndembu ritual and arguing that it 'does not reflect or express ... the structure of a stable society'[50], but instead 'it compensates for the integrational deficiencies of a practically unstable society'.[51] This compensation is achieved through the use of symbols: 'In the context of the ritual the common values of the whole society are stressed in symbol, mime and precept.'[52] In a lecture delivered in 1958 Turner discussed these symbols in greater detail, suggesting that they have what he referred to as an ideological and a sensory pole. At the ideological pole 'is found a cluster of *significata* that refer to components of the moral and social orders of Ndembu society'.[53] At the sensory pole 'the *significata* are usually natural and physiological phenomena and processes'.[54]

In another lecture, delivered in 1963 and discussing the use of colour symbolism in Ndembu ritual, he suggested that the sensory, individual pole was prior to the ideological, social one: 'Not only do the three colours stand for basic human experiences of the body (associated with the gratification of libido, hunger, aggressive and excretory drives, and with fear, anxiety, and submissiveness), they also provide a kind of primordial classification of reality.'[55] As he emphasises, this view puts him in opposition to Durkheim's argument that social structure is the first classificatory system: 'Against this I would postulate that the human organism and its crucial experiences are the *fons et origo* of all classifications.'[56]

In *The Drums of Affliction*, published in 1968, Turner examines Ndembu ritual in greater detail. He begins by describing Ndembu religious beliefs. These are in an otiose high god; in ancestor spirits with a power to bestow or withhold the good things of life; in medicines with an intrinsic efficacy that can be released by a ritual practitioner; and in the destructive power of witches and sorcerers. He defines Ndembu ritual as follows: 'By "rite" or "ritual" I mean, when referring to Ndembu culture, prescribed formal behaviour not given over to technological routine, having reference to beliefs in mystical (or non-empirical) beings or powers.'[57]

The symbols used in ritual are again characterised as having both a sensory and an ideological pole: 'In ritual symbols proper those *significata* which represent emotionally-charged phenomena and processes, such as blood, milk, semen, and faeces, are fused and condensed with *significata* which stand for aspects of social virtue.'[58] Thus mother's milk, symbolised by a tree which exudes white sap, fuses the infantile pleasure of breast-feeding with the social principle of matrilineage, that is the practice of tracing descent through the female line: 'It would seem that the needs of the individual biopsychical organism and the needs of society, in many respects opposed, come to terms with one another in the master-symbols of Ndembu society.'[59]

Turner suggests that Ndembu ritual resolves the opposition between the sensory and the ideological in other, cathartic ways. As he puts it: 'Ritual also recognises that the psychic nature of man is not infinitely malleable with respect to the forces of social conditioning. To make a human being obey social norms, violence must be done to his natural impulses.'[60] Thus 'ritual must give expression to the illicit drives, bring them into the open, as the Ndembu say themselves, in order that they may be purged and exorcised'.[61] Turner also emphasises the dramatic nature of such public catharsis: 'This notion of "drama" is crucial to the understanding of ritual.'[62]

A lecture delivered in 1964 indicated the wider range of Turner's concerns. In this lecture he concentrated on the transition stage identified by van Gennep in his analysis of rites of passage, discussing this aspect of Ndembu ritual in relation to similar rituals in other societies.

He referred to this stage, and to the people in it, as 'interstructural',[63] and like Douglas described it as contrary to classification and powerful. In *The Ritual Process*, published in 1969 and perhaps Turner's best known work, he develops this theme, presenting a more elaborate interpretation of van Gennep's tripartite structure. He describes the first stage as separation of the ritual participant from everyday consciousness or social position; the second stage as provision of a moment of liminality, a psychological and social state of transition in which sacred power is encountered; and the third stage as reintegration of the ritual participant into everyday life with a new status. He stresses the powerful nature of liminality: 'Liminal situations and roles are almost everywhere attributed with magico-religious powers.'[64] He also argues that liminality is not restricted to a stage in ritual, suggesting that in religions such as Christianity it has become a permanent condition.

For Turner liminality is also associated with egalitarianism in that a ritual initiate is on an equal status with any fellow initiates participating in the ritual. He refers to this type of social relationship as communitas, a type of social levelling and bonding which he distinguishes from structure. While he regards communitas as being most characteristically expressed in liminality, he also regards it as occurring outside liminality, in a wide range of marginal social groups such as monks, holy fools and subjugated aboriginal peoples, and more generally as a form of social experience which interacts with its opposite, structure: 'For individuals and groups, social life is a type of dialectical process that involves successive experience of ... communitas and structure, homogeneity and differentiation, equality and inequality.'[65]

Tambiah

While many of the scholars discussed in this chapter have been mainly interested in religion, three recent publications by the anthropologist S. J. Tambiah have focused on the nature of magic, describing it primarily as a rhetorical art and again incorporating it within the category of the symbolic as distinct from the scientific.

Tambiah begins an article published in 1973 by arguing that it is inappropriate to judge magic in scientific terms. In doing so he adopts a distinction developed in linguistic philosophy between descriptive utterances which can be judged as either true or false and performative utterances (discussed previously in relation to the phenomenological approach of Smart) in which an action is 'performed' by virtue of having been spoken, for example saying 'I declare this road open' opens the road, and which are often accompanied by symbolically appropriate manipulation of an object, such as cutting a ribbon.

As Tambiah puts it: 'Magical acts are ritual acts, and ritual acts are in turn performative acts whose positive and creative meaning is missed and whose persuasive validity is misjudged if they are subjected to that kind of empirical verification associated with scientific activity.'[66] He describes performative acts as ones 'which simply by virtue of being enacted (under the appropriate conditions) achieve a change of state, or do something effective (for example, an installation ceremony undergone by the candidate makes him a "chief")'.[67] The appropriate conditions include such factors as the act being performed by an accredited person and according to the proper conventions. As another example of a performative act he refers to a wedding ceremony in which a man says he takes a woman to be his lawful wedded wife: 'The uttering of the sentence cannot merely be described as saying something, but is, or is a part of, the *doing of an action*.'[68]

Tambiah regards magic as being primarily concerned with transferring a desirable property to a recipient lacking that property. In addition to being a performative act, such transfer involves what he refers to as persuasive analogy: 'Magical acts, usually compounded of verbal utterance and object manipulation, constitute "performative" acts by which a property is imperatively transferred to a recipient object or person on an analogical basis.'[69] He describes persuasive analogy as depending on a recognition of both the similarities and the differences between two items, and thus as involving both positive and negative analogy.

As an example of persuasive analogy he discusses the statement that 'the employer is to his workers as a father is to his children'.[70] Here there is a positive analogy, for example in terms of economic dependence, between the workers' relation to their employer and the children's to their father. But there is also a negative analogy in that, for example, a father loves his children: 'It is precisely this expansion of meaning or the transfer of these additional values to the employer-worker relation that is sought by invoking the father-children analogy.'[71]

For an example of persuasive analogy from magic Tambiah turns to the Zande medicines discussed by Evans-Pritchard. On a positive level there is an analogy between, for example, the Zande medicine for leprosy and the patient: the medicine comes from a plant that sheds its leaves as a leper sheds limb-extremities. But there is also a negative analogy: the plant's leaves grow again while the leper may die. It is this additional and desirable property that the ritual aims to transfer to the leper, a transfer that 'represents symbolic, not causal, action'.[72]

In these Zande medical rituals there is a complementary relationship between verbal utterance and object manipulation, with the recitation specifying the desirable quality that is to be transferred while at the same time the ritual object, the medicine, is brought into contact with the recipient. Tambiah describes magic in general in similar terms:

> The rite consists in persuasively transferring the properties of the desired and desirable ... to the other which is in an undesirable condition, or in attempting to convert a potential, not-yet-achieved state into an actualized one. The manipulation is made operationally realistic by directing the transfer not only by word but, as in the Zande case, by bringing a material piece of the object in the desirable-desired analogy into contact with the object in need of transfer.[73]

In an earlier article published in 1968, Tambiah argues that magic features more types of recitation, often in an ordered sequence, than Frazer's model of coercion suggests: commanding spells as well as invocations, supplications, mythological narratives and descriptive statements of effects. In addition, he makes a distinction between two ways of analysing magic. One is in terms of its outer pragmatic frame, that is the ends towards which it is directed. Here he distinguishes between prospective and retrospective magic: prospective magic, for example fertility rituals, is a stimulus or signal of a subsequent event, a celebration of the regularity of that event; retrospective magic, for example therapeutic rituals that attribute illness to witchcraft, explains and counters irregularity in events. The second way of analysing magic is in terms of its inner semantic frame, that is the logic by which it represents a transfer of desirable properties.

In relation to inner-frame analysis, he argues that magic is a heightened use of language complemented by appropriate actions or object manipulations which realistically imitate practical techniques. As he puts it: 'A close analysis of Trobriand ritual [originally studied by Malinowski] shows that it actively exploits the expressive powers of language, the sensory qualities of objects, and the instrumental properties of action simultaneously in a number of ways.'[74] To illustrate magic's exploitation of the expressive properties of language, Tambiah compares Frazer's two types of sympathetic magic, homeopathic and contagious, to two types of figurative speech: metaphor, for example when a king is said to be a lion in battle, and metonymy, for example when a crown represents a king. He argues that both homeopathic magic and metaphor can be viewed as fusing together two things which are in some way similar, and that both contagious magic and metonymy can be viewed as displacing one thing on to another thing which is contiguous.

As an example of inner-frame analysis, Tambiah discusses a Trobriand cultivation recitation, 'The belly of my garden grows to the size of a bush-hen's nest', which is accompanied by the rubbing of soil from a hen's breeding nest onto an adze. He describes how the recitation sets up a metaphor between the nest and the garden while the action consists of transferring the desired property, the size of the nest, to the adze by rubbing it with soil metonymically connected to the nest. The adze then transfers this desired property to the garden. As he puts it: 'The rite of transfer portrays a metaphorical use of language (verbal substitution) whereby an attribute is transferred to the recipient via a material symbol which is used metonymically as a transformer.'[75] Thus the expressive properties of language are combined with the instrumental properties of action: 'The technique gains its realism by clothing a metaphorical procedure in the operational or manipulative mode of practical action; it unites both concept and action, word and deed.'[76]

Tambiah's *Magic, Science, Religion and the Scope of Rationality*, published in 1990, is, as its title suggests, a more wide-ranging study of the nature of magic. Tambiah begins this book by arguing that the distinctions made by the early intellectualists between magic and religion reflected two aspects of their heritage. One influence was the distinction developed in early Judaism – and maintained in the Bible – between true religion and false religion, regarded as pagan idolatry or magic. In the terms of the Bible the true religion is one in which God created nature from nothing, so the division between God and nature is wide; God also controls nature so misfortune is thought to be divine punishment. In contrast, what the Bible regards as magic are religions in which pagan deities are rooted in nature and misfortune is thought to be caused by autonomous forces operating in nature.

The second influence on the intellectualists, Tambiah suggests, was the distinction developed in the late sixteenth and early seventeenth centuries by English Protestant propagandists 'between religious acts as primarily intercessionary in character, and magical acts as being coercive rituals ambitiously attempting to coerce the divine'.[77] Tambiah argues that this represents a further step: the Protestant propagandists 'not only declare magic to be a false religion, they also declare it to be inefficacious action, for the true God cannot be so manipulated'.[78]

Tambiah thinks these negative assessments of magic contributed towards the intellectualists describing it as crudely rational. He suggests instead that it is better 'to move away from seeing magic as "bad science" to seeing it as "rhetorical art"'.[79] He leaves open, however, 'the puzzle posed by magic by virtue of its "duality"'[80] in that on the one hand it is rhetorical and performative while on the other it imitates the logic of technical actions that seek to transform nature.

Tambiah also returns to the question of two contrasting modes of thought, here favouring the terms causal and participatory. He associates the former primarily with science, and the latter primarily with magic, religion and art. However, rather than these being modes of thought, Tambiah suggests that they are socially constructed orientations to reality, and that the context in which each operates, and the factors prompting a switch from one to the other, require further study: 'It is this context in which sacred attitudes are evoked and in which code switching occurs that remains for us still a major phenomenon to interpret.'[81]

Geertz

Like Durkheim, the American anthropologist Clifford Geertz is one of the few scholars to have advanced a definition of religion that does not feature a belief in deities. This definition, developed in an article published in 1966, is perhaps the one most often used in anthropology after Tylor's. While Durkheim stressed the influence of social structure on religion, in this article Geertz stresses the influence of religion on social structure, describing religion as a symbolic system which brings a sense of cosmic order to existence and shapes our perception of reality.

An earlier article published in 1959 provides some indication of Geertz's approach, generally referred to as interpretive and regarded as continuing in the tradition of Weber. In this article Geertz develops a distinction between three elements in human behaviour. One is psychological, that is 'the pattern of motivational integration within the individual which we usually call personality structure'.[82] The other two are culture system and social structure; on one hand 'there is the framework of beliefs, expressive symbols, and values in terms of which individuals define their world, express their feelings, and make their judgements',[83] on the other 'there is the ongoing process of interactive behaviour, whose persistent form we call social structure'.[84] In addition, he argues that discontinuities between culture system and social structure represent 'some of the primary driving forces in change'.[85]

In his 1966 article Geertz offers a definition of religion that attempts to incorporate these three elements:

> A religion is (1) a system of symbols which acts to (2) establish powerful, pervasive, and long-lasting moods and motivations in men by (3) formulating conceptions of a general order of existence and (4) clothing these conceptions with such an aura of factuality that (5) the moods and motivations seem uniquely realistic.[86]

In discussing the first part of his definition, that religion is a system of symbols, Geertz defines symbols as 'any object, act, event, quality, or relation which serves as a vehicle for a conception – the conception is the symbol's "meaning"'.[87] He regards such symbols, and the culture systems that include them, as both shaping our perception of reality and being shaped by it: 'Culture patterns have an intrinsic double aspect: they give meaning, that is objective conceptual form, to social and psychological reality both by shaping themselves to it and by shaping it to themselves.'[88] He argues similarly that religion is sociologically interesting not because 'it describes the social order (which, in so far as it does, it does not only very obliquely but very incompletely), but because ... it shapes it'.[89] This shaping power of symbols relates to the second part of Geertz's definition, that religious symbols establish powerful and pervasive moods and motivations in people.

Continuing to the third part of his definition, that religion formulates conceptions of order, Geertz describes religious symbols as having such a strong effect on people's moods and motivations because they provide a cosmic framework of order, that is they are 'symbolic of some transcendent truths'.[90] For Geertz there are three principal threats to this cosmic order, 'three points where chaos – a tumult of events which lack not just interpretations but *interpretability* – threatens to break in upon man'[91]. These points are 'at the limits of his analytic capacities, at the limits of his powers of endurance, and at the limits of his moral insight'.[92] Geertz relates the first point to intellectualist interpretations of religion as explanatory, the second to Malinowski's emotionalist interpretation and the third to Weber's theodicean interpretation.

The fourth part of Geertz's definition, that religion clothes these conceptions of order with an aura of factuality, relates primarily to ritual: 'It is in some sort of ceremonial form ... that the moods and motivations which sacred symbols induce in men and the general conceptions of the order of existence which they formulate for men meet and reinforce one another.'[93] Similarly it is in ritual that 'an aura of utter actuality'[94] is created.

The final part of Geertz's definition, that religion establishes moods and motivations that seem uniquely realistic, to a degree again raises the question of two contrasting modes of thought, in Geertz's terms the religious and the common-sense. However, Geertz regards the two more as orientations to reality, adding that the religious orientation can transform the common-sense orientation. He argues that because ritual gives conceptions of order such a strong aura of factuality, people's perceptions of reality are altered, as is their behaviour. As Geertz puts it:

> Having ritually 'leapt' ... into the framework of meaning which religious conceptions define, and the ritual ended, returned again to the common-sense world, a man is ... changed. And as he is changed, so also is the common-sense world, for it is now seen as but the partial form of a wider reality which corrects and completes it.[95]

He suggests similarly that ritual alters 'the whole landscape presented to common sense, alters it in such a way that the moods and motivations induced by religious practice seem themselves supremely practical, the only sensible ones to adopt given the way things "really" are'.[96]

Notes

1. Lévy-Bruhl 1926: 23.
2. Lévy-Bruhl 1926: 23.
3. Lévy-Bruhl 1926: 27.
4. Lévy-Bruhl 1926: 38.
5. Lévy-Bruhl 1926: 40.
6. Lévy-Bruhl 1926: 44.
7. Lévy-Bruhl 1926: 60.
8. Lévy-Bruhl 1926: 68.

9. Lévy-Bruhl 1926: 77.
10. Lévy-Bruhl 1926: 382.
11. Van Gennep 1960: 13.
12. Douglas 1970: 12.
13. Douglas 1970: 15.
14. Douglas 1970: 14.
15. Douglas 1970: 14.
16. Douglas 1970: 30.
17. Douglas 1970: 35.
18. Douglas 1970: 74.
19. Douglas 1970: 110.
20. Douglas 1970: 111.
21. Douglas 1970: 30.
22. Douglas 1970: 34.
23. Douglas 1970: 84–5.
24. Douglas 1970: 85.
25. Douglas 1970: 84.
26. Douglas 1970: 85.
27. Douglas 1970: 89.
28. Douglas 1970: 84.
29. Douglas 1970: 196.
30. Douglas 1970: 114.
31. Douglas 1970: 116.
32. Douglas 1970: 138.
33. Douglas 1970: 148.
34. Douglas 1970: 193.
35. Douglas 1973: 12.
36. Douglas 1973: 12.
37. Douglas 1973: 28.
38. Douglas 1973: 26.
39. Douglas 1973: 81.
40. Douglas 1973: 87.
41. Douglas 1973: 144.
42. Douglas 1973: 193.
43. Douglas 1973: 193.
44. Douglas 1975a: 56.
45. Van Gennep 1960: 13.
46. Beattie 1970: 242.
47. Beattie 1970: 245.
48. Beattie 1970: 240.
49. Beattie 1970: 240.
50. Turner 1957: xxi.

51. Turner 1957: xxi.
52. Turner 1957: xxi.
53. Turner 1967a: 28.
54. Turner 1967a: 28.
55. Turner 1967b: 89–90.
56. Turner 1967b: 89–90.
57. Turner 1968: 15.
58. Turner 1968: 44.
59. Turner 1968: 19.
60. Turner 1968: 235–6.
61. Turner 1968: 236.
62. Turner 1968: 273.
63. Turner 1967c: 93.
64. Turner 1969: 108.
65. Turner 1969: 97.
66. Tambiah 1985b: 60.
67. Tambiah 1985b: 79.
68. Tambiah 1985b: 78.
69. Tambiah 1985b: 60.
70. Tambiah 1985b: 71.
71. Tambiah 1985b: 71.
72. Tambiah 1985b: 74.
73. Tambiah 1985b: 72.
74. Tambiah 1985a: 37.
75. Tambiah 1985a: 43.
76. Tambiah 1985a: 43.
77. Tambiah 1990: 19.
78. Tambiah 1990: 19–20.
79. Tambiah 1990: 82.
80. Tambiah 1990: 82.
81. Tambiah 1990: 92.
82. Geertz 1993a: 145.
83. Geertz 1993a: 145.
84. Geertz 1993a: 145.
85. Geertz 1993a: 144.
86. Geertz 1993b: 90.
87. Geertz 1993b: 91.
88. Geertz 1993b: 93.
89. Geertz 1993b: 119.
90. Geertz 1993b: 98.
91. Geertz 1993b: 100.
92. Geertz 1993b: 100.

93. Geertz 1993b: 112.
94. Geertz 1993b: 112.
95. Geertz 1993b: 122.
96. Geertz 1993b: 122.

7
·
Recent intellectualist approaches
·

D ESPITE ATTEMPTS BY THE likes of Durkheim and Geertz to define religion in terms that do not require a belief in spiritual beings, many British anthropologists since the Second World War have favoured the earlier intellectualist definition. Such anthropologists have also favoured the intellectualist description of religion as an explanatory model, that is as a method of explaining events by attributing them to divine intervention. However, they have restated the earlier intellectualist position in a slightly broader way. Frazer and his colleagues primarily regarded magic as a method of controlling events and religion as a means of explanation that arose when it was realised that events were outside human control. In addition to abandoning this evolutionist framework, post-war intellectualists regard magic as a means both of controlling events and of explaining them through attribution to magical agency, and similarly regard religion as a method both of explaining events and of influencing them through appeals either for helpful divine intervention or against its harmful equivalent.

This emphasis on magic and religion as explanatory models brings another method of explaining events – science – into the intellectualists' discussions of the sacred and leads them to oppose the distinction made by other anthropologists between two modes of thought. In addition, the emphasis on magic and religion as methods of influencing events, that is on the explicit functions of ritual, puts them in opposition to the symbolist emphasis on the implicit functions of ritual. Various examples of this intellectualist revival are discussed in this chapter: Goody's rejection of Durkheim's categories and advocacy of the earlier intellectualists' definitions of magic and religion;

various publications by Jarvie and Horton that attack the idea of two contrasting modes of thought; and Skorupski's broader discussion of the nature of religion and of sympathetic magic.

Goody

In an article published in 1961, Jack Goody rejects Durkheim's distinctions between magic and religion, and between the sacred and profane, advocating a return to the intellectualists' categories. In rejecting Durkheim's distinction between magic and religion, Goody argues that magic can be as collective as religion:

> Magic is no less a social phenomenon, in the strict sense, than religion. Sorcery, for example, depends for its effects upon a certain degree of consensus, upon the acceptance of a set of social norms by a significant proportion of the members of a society.[1]

Goody also rejects 'Durkheim's assumption that the sacred-profane dichotomy is a universal feature of people's views of the human situation'.[2] He argues that the ethnographic evidence, that is the evidence of the beliefs and practices of various societies, suggests the opposite and that the sacred and profane are 'inextricably intertwined'.[3]

He recommends instead a version of the intellectualists' definition of magic, modified in that he refers to irrationality rather than crude rationality, and of religion, relating it to the involvement of spiritual beings. First he defines ritual: 'In conclusion then, by ritual we refer to a category of standardised behaviour (custom) in which the relationship between the means and the end is not "intrinsic", i.e. is either irrational or non-rational.'[4] Magic is one part of ritual: 'Within this general category falls magical action, which is essentially irrational, since it has a pragmatic end which its procedures fail to achieve, or achieve for other reasons than the patient, and possibly the practitioner, supposes. This is Frazer's "bastard science".'[5] In contrast 'there are religious acts, which may be irrational (as in the case of many forms of sacrifice and prayer) or they may be non-rational, as in many public celebrations, but all of which involve supernatural beings'.[6]

Jarvie

The question of what constitutes rationality is far from straightforward and has been discussed by I. C. Jarvie who also favours the intellectualist perception of, and distinction between, religion and magic. As a result of interpreting religion and magic as explanatory models, Jarvie argues that the two have some similarities to science.

In *The Revolution in Anthropology*, published in 1964, Jarvie discusses the nature of millenarian religion (that is religions that seek salvation and social transformation, named after Biblical predictions of Christ's second coming and rule for one thousand years) and more specifically cargo cults (religions in the south-west Pacific which expect spirits to bring believers material goods or cargoes). He advances an intellectualist interpretation of the cargo cults: 'The structure of their doctrines indicates what is wanted and they are attempts to provide an explanation of why they haven't got it and a religious prescription for how they can get it.'[7] He indicates that this interpretation aligns him with Frazer: 'There is in my position a defence of Frazer's doctrine that there is the following close relationship between magic, science and religion. They are all attempts to explain and control the world.'[8]

Jarvie argues further that magical and religious actions are rational in two senses. Firstly, they are rational in the context of a society's beliefs:

> My theory of millenarian religion in general and therefore of cargo cult religion in particular is a rational one. I attribute reasonable aims to the actors in the situation and try to show that, within their frame of reference, their actions, if interpreted as trying to realise these aims, are perfectly rational.[9]

Secondly, they are rational because they are directed towards a goal, 'accepting the idea of goal-directedness as the criterion of rationality'.[10]

In a more general article written in collaboration with Joseph Agassi and published in 1967, Jarvie refines this definition of rationality, distinguishing between weak rationality, magic and religion, on the one hand and strong rationality, science, on the other. Both weak and strong rationality are goal-directed but only in strong rationality is action based on a belief that 'satisfies some standard or criterion of rationality which has been adopted, such as that it is based on good evidence, or is beyond reasonable doubt, or is held open to criticism, etc.'.[11] This article is specifically directed against symbolist approaches that read 'social values into the symbolism of magic',[12] arguing that such approaches ignore the reasons people perform magic, that is the goals towards which it is directed.

In *Rationality and Relativism*, published in 1984, Jarvie continues to challenge 'those anthropologists who try to make a case for some qualitative difference between systems of superstitious thought and science'.[13] He also discusses Frazer's distinction between magic, religion and science:

> The labels are simply analytical distinctions best employed in the manner suggested by Frazer. This rough and ready distinction turns on whether the causal agents thought to be at work are manipulable animated natural forces, in which case we call it 'magic'; personalised supernatural forces, in which case we call it 'religion'; or impersonal, inanimate natural forces, in which case we call it 'science'.[14]

Jarvie also suggests that the three can be mixed: 'There are strong magical and religious elements in science, both content and practice; and the same goes for magic and religion.'[15] Having conceded the religious and magical side of science, he hopes that 'perhaps now the cognitive and technological claims of magic and religion can be faced too'.[16]

Horton

In an article published in 1967, Robin Horton also proposes a continuity between religion and science in that both are explanatory. However, unlike Jarvie, and unlike the earlier intellectualists who argued that magic and science are similar because both assume invariable processes in nature, he contrasts magic with science. Horton describes African religions as offering an explanatory theory, that is as postulating theoretical entities that link events to causes as science does: 'Both are making the same use of theory to transcend the limited vision of natural causes provided by common sense.'[17] Consequently he argues that it is misleading to contrast religion and science as different modes of thought. Instead the difference is better described in terms of attitude to theory: in oral societies this is closed, in scientifically-oriented societies, open. Magic, according to Horton, is different to both religion and science, being described as primarily a belief in the power of words, that is a belief that in certain contexts words have a magical power 'to bring into being the events or states they stand for'.[18]

In an article published in 1973, Horton returns to the subject of two contrasting modes of thought. He suggests there is an ambiguity in Durkheim's treatment of religion in *The Elementary Forms of the Religious Life*. On the one hand there is a contrast between the sacred and the profane; on the other hand there is a continuity in that religion classifies nature and thus gives rise to scientific thought. He argues that the model of contrast, expressed in various terms, has been followed by most anthropologists, while the model of continuity, which he associates with the intellectualist approach, has been unjustly neglected. He suggests that this neglect reflects, among other things, a liberal reluctance to describe oral societies as less advanced than Western. Instead such societies are romanticised as more symbolic: 'We can at last understand the strange antics of the social anthropologist who refuses to take traditional explanations at their face value.'[19]

Skorupski

In *Symbol and Theory*, published in 1976, John Skorupski examines the dispute between intellectualist and symbolist approaches to religion, broadly favouring the literalism of the intellectualist approach, that is its willingness in Horton's terms to take traditional explanations at their face value. In this book Skorupski also provides a reassessment of Frazer's two categories of sympathetic magic – homeopathic and contagious – and discusses magic's relationship to performative acts, a concept developed in linguistic philosophy and discussed previously in relation to the work of two other scholars, Smart's phenomenological approach and Tambiah's symbolic approach.

Skorupski describes the intellectualists' interpretation of religion as consisting of four elements: religious actions are to be understood in terms of the participants' beliefs that give them a rationale; these beliefs are acquired by socialisation; they continue to be held because of blocks to their falsification; and they originate 'out of a need to understand and control the natural environment'.[20]

He describes as literalist a view that concurs with this but accepts 'that there are important needs and pre-occupations, significantly different from the activist, this-worldly ones of explanation and control, which from the first shape and form the content of religious thought'.[21] As he puts it:

On a literalist approach it does become clear that, as the intellectualist claims, in traditional cultures religious beliefs are often brought in in contexts of prediction and explanation, and religious actions are often performed with the aim of controlling natural events. Of course it does not follow that explanation, prediction and control are the primary or primitive functions of religious belief and action.[22]

Examples of the other functions and beliefs of religion to which he refers include doctrines of the after-life and of salvation, that is deliverance from sin and the divine punishment consequent upon it. Skorupski also indicates that, rather than being concerned only with explanation, religion can involve paradox or mystery, pointing to 'the paradoxical character of such doctrines as the Trinity, the Eucharist and the Incarnation'.[23] He suggests similarly that 'in a number of African religions areas of paradox ... can be found which seem structurally analogous to the paradoxes involved in the Catholic doctrines'.[24]

Skorupski rejects Durkheim's definition of religion and favours Frazer's: a belief in spiritual beings and a primary practice of propitiating them. To include within this definition religions such as Buddhism, which place less emphasis on spiritual beings, he suggests that these two criteria be regarded as sufficient but not necessary. Skorupski also rejects Durkheim's distinction between religion as collective and magic as individualist, arguing that it fails to recognise that such an opposition 'does not exist as a general fact'.[25] Instead he again accepts Frazer's distinction, that magic does not feature a belief in spiritual beings, or if it does so coerces those beings rather than propitiates them, conceding that it is often difficult to distinguish a magical command from a religious request.

However, Skorupski expresses reservations about Frazer's principles of sympathetic magic – homeopathic magic obeying the law of similarity and contagious magic obeying the law of contact – arguing that Frazer's theory 'is vaguely stated and further confused by the heterogeneity of the examples he gives'.[26] For example, he queries: 'Does the [homeopathic] dictum that "like produces like" mean that a like change in one object produces a like change in another? Presumably not – for this applies equally to *contagious* transfer.'[27] Instead he suggests a modified classification of magic, symbolic identification and contagious transfer.

In contagious transfer a property of an initial object is transferred to a goal-object. Thus, for example, the growth-property of a berry is spat on a child. Skorupski argues that this is covered neither by homeopathy, for the berry is not like the child, nor by contagion, for the two have not previously been in contact.

In symbolic identification a change in a symbol of a goal-object produces a change in the goal-object. Thus, for example, burning a person's effigy or hair burns the person represented by the effigy or formerly connected with the hair. Skorupski stresses here the importance of identification: 'The symbol in some sense is, or participates in, the reality it represents.'[28] He compares this to the Catholic mass:

> The traditional Catholic can tell as well as anybody between the host he eats and that received by his fellow communicant. But he nevertheless believes that each is the living body of Christ. There is no sharp distinction made here between the symbol as mere representation, on the one hand, and as manifestation, or revelation, on the other.[29]

Contagious transfer and symbolic identification can be combined, a property of an initial object being transferred to a symbol of a goal-object and so to the goal-object. Thus, for example, the technical proficiency of a father is transferred to a navel string he wears round his wrist; the navel string symbolises his son, so the proficiency is transferred to the son.

Skorupski next discusses the relationship between magic and performative acts, or what he refers to more broadly as operative actions such as electing someone to a peerage: 'The point of each of these operative actions is to bring about a consequence, which takes effect when the action is performed in due form by the right person(s). Thus a sentence is passed, a verdict delivered or a will made, and duly takes effect.'[30] He suggests that magic appears to be similar to such operative actions: 'It is not difficult to feel some kind of connexion here with those conventionalised operative actions which comprise a set performative utterance ("I declare this road open") with an appropriate "performative" symbolic action (cutting a ribbon).'[31]

However, he thinks that on his interpretation so far magic is distinct from operative action:

> The symbolic enactments which often accompany magical spells are seen from the point of view of the 'operative theory' as non-verbal ways of saying what is said in the spell. On the identificationist view of symbolic magic, on the other hand, they are seen as ways of acting on the goal-object itself by acting on the symbol which manifests it. The latter theory is more in tune with a wider body of cross-cultural ethnographic evidence.[32]

But magic can be incorporated within operative theory if it is interpreted as a way of triggering a consequential action, that is as 'a way of signalling what is being done and thereby doing it'.[33]

Skorupski also discusses operative theory in relation to interpretation of the Christian sacraments as channels through which divine grace is imparted. He argues that baptism can be classified as operative if it is interpreted as a sign that the subject is cleansed from sin and constituted as a member of the Church. However, he suggests that the emphasis in baptism on an ontological change in the soul, that is on a change in the soul's being, is magical rather than operative: 'In as much as it [baptism] is conceived to have an ontological effect on the soul rather than being thought to have a purely operative character, it still has the characteristics of what is commonly discussed under the heading of "magical action".'[34]

Skorupski discusses in similar terms the doctrine that the body of Christ is present in the consecrated bread and wine: 'No interpretation of it as an *operatively* efficacious symbolic act is consistent with doctrines of the Real Presence, in particular with Transubstantiation. It has the appearance of a magical binding or a localisation of the god in a physical thing.'[35] He continues: 'With this as with other sacraments the Catholic defence against accusations of magic was not that the power of sacraments was operative rather than causal: but that the causal power was God-given and hence could not be said to bind God.'[36]

Skorupski also discusses the similarity proposed by Frazer between magic and science, that both assume invariable processes in nature, and the similarity proposed by Horton between religion and science, that both are explanatory models. He rejects Frazer's comparison between magic and science, and his separation of religion from these two:

> His 'sympathetic' account of magic is incorrect, but even if correct would not support the comparison between science and magic which he wants to make. Nor is his ground for taking religion as the odd-man-out particularly convincing, at least when considered in the light of the characteristically this-worldly preoccupations of a primitive religion.[37]

Instead Skorupski finds Horton's comparison between religion and science 'considerably more fertile'.[38]

Notes
.

1. Goody 1961: 146–7.
2. Goody 1961: 155.
3. Goody 1961: 151.
4. Goody 1961: 159.
5. Goody 1961: 159.
6. Goody 1961: 159.
7. Jarvie 1964: 67.
8. Jarvie 1964: 67.
9 Jarvie 1964: 131.
10. Jarvie 1964: 132.
11. Jarvie and Agassi 1970: 173.
12. Jarvie and Agassi 1970: 183.
13. Jarvie 1984: 34.
14. Jarvie 1984: 51.
15. Jarvie 1984: 51.
16. Jarvie 1984: 37.
17. Horton 1970: 136.
18. Horton 1970: 155.
19. Horton 1973: 294.
20. Skorupski 1976: 9.
21. Skorupski 1976: 11.
22. Skorupski 1976: 206.
23. Skorupski 1976: 218.
24. Skorupski 1976: 219.
25. Skorupski 1976: 127.
26. Skorupski 1976: 136.
27. Skorupski 1976: 136.
28. Skorupski 1976: 144.
29. Skorupski 1976: 144.
30. Skorupski 1976: 152.
31. Skorupski 1976: 152.
32. Skorupski 1976: 152.
33. Skorupski 1976: 153.
34. Skorupski 1976: 127.
35. Skorupski 1976: 110.
36. Skorupski 1976: 110.
37. Skorupski 1976: 182–3.
38. Skorupski 1976: 182.

8

·

Structural approaches

·

I N FRANCE MUCH OF the work of Durkheim's school of sociology
was brought to an end by the First World War, with the particular
exception of Mauss whose career continued, less concerned with the
sacred but maintaining an interest in classificatory systems. Durkheim's influence was further reduced by the establishment of existentialism as the dominant philosophical movement in France. This
philosophy bore the imprint of phenomenology and was concerned
with studying certain extreme states of consciousness that it associated
with the human situation in the world, such as an awareness of the
inevitability of death and of the indefinite nature of human identity,
arguing that such identity is achieved through acts of choice and that
the particular characteristic of human existence is that people always
face such choices. A further influence on existentialism was the work
of the nineteenth-century Danish theologian and philosopher Søren
Kierkegaard (1813–55) which was directly opposed to the philosophy
of Hegel with which this book began. While Hegel regarded *Geist* as
a spiritual unity encompassing people and nature, Kierkegaard con-
trasted human existence with the kind of existence possessed by the
rest of nature and stressed a distinctness between God and people,
arguing that belief in God requires an act of choice similar to those
discussed by existentialists.

However, the influence of Durkheim, in particular his emphasis on
the structuring properties of classificatory systems that affect our perception of the world, was revived in the structuralism that eclipsed
existentialism after the Second World War and one of whose major
figures was Lévi-Strauss, France's leading anthropologist in this period. Structuralism involves a complex set of theories, most impor-

tantly an argument that culture consists of communication systems that can be interpreted in the same way as language, regarded as the primary communication system. More specifically structuralists argue that culture can be interpreted according to principles developed in what is referred to as Saussurean linguistics. This type of linguistics, named after the Swiss linguist Ferdinand de Saussure (1857–1913) and further developed by the post-war linguist Roman Jakobson, emphasises a distinction between *langue* (language) and *parole* (speech), with *langue* being the underlying structuring system, that is the body of linguistic rules that speakers must follow in order to communicate, and *parole* being the structured manifestations of *langue*, that is the day-to-day use made of the structuring system.

Structural anthropologists argue that cultural phenomena also have an underlying structuring system whose characteristics they seek to identify. Despite the similarities in terminology there is therefore a major difference between the social structuralism of Durkheim and the structuralism of Lévi-Strauss: while Durkheim regarded religious structure as being grounded in social structure, Lévi-Strauss regarded both as being grounded in the unconscious structuring activities of the mind.

The subject of religion is discussed less frequently in structural anthropology than in other types of anthropology. However, structuralism's importance as an approach to the study of culture deserves consideration in a book such as this. While this chapter concentrates on the work of Lévi-Strauss, two other post-war scholars are also discussed: the British anthropologist Leach whose career includes a period during which he adopted a structural approach, and the French anthropologist Godelier whose structural Marxism both indicates the continuing influence of Marx in the twentieth century and responds to some of the criticisms that have been levelled at Lévi-Strauss's structuralism.

Leach

Edmund Leach's long career provides a link between two major developments in twentieth-century anthropology: the pioneering work of Malinowski, who established the importance of fieldwork to anthropology and taught Leach at the London School of Economics, and the interest in structuralism as a theoretical framework for interpreting data such as that gathered in fieldwork, a framework favoured by Leach in some of his publications. However, this is not intended to imply that the process of acquiring data, through fieldwork and other means, is independent of the process of interpretation, because choice of theoretical approach is likely to affect choice both of data and of the questions asked of that data.

Three particular publications by Leach are discussed in this section, one dating from the 1950s and studying a specific society, a more general introduction to anthropology dating from the 1970s and reflecting the influence of structuralism, and another general introduction, dating from the 1980s, in which the influence of structuralism is less evident.

Leach's *Political Systems of Highland Burma*, published in 1954, continues the discussion of the relationship between ritual and social structure which has been one of the central topics in British anthropology under the influence of Durkheim. Leach argues that, in the case of the Burmese communities studied, 'ritual makes explicit the social structure'.[1] But more specifically he suggests that it makes explicit an ideal rather than a real structure: 'The individuals who make up a society must from time to time be reminded, at least in symbol, of the underlying order that is supposed to guide their social activities.'[2] This distinction between real and ideal social structures enables Leach to describe change in terms of relations between the two, thus avoiding the type of static view of a society suggested by a perception of ritual and social structure as perfectly matched.

In this book Leach relates ritual primarily to the sacred, describing it in terms reminiscent of discussions of two contrasting modes of thought: 'At one extreme we have actions which are entirely profane, entirely functional, technique pure and simple; at the other we have actions which are entirely sacred, strictly aesthetic, technically non-functional.'[3] However, he argues that ritual is an aspect of most behaviour:

> Between these two extremes we have the great majority of social actions which partly partake of the one sphere and partly of the other. From this point of view technique and ritual, profane and sacred, do not denote *types* of action but *aspects* of almost any kind of action.[4]

To express this in slightly different terms, social behaviour can thus be viewed as having two aspects: one instrumental and aiming to do something and the other symbolic and expressing something about the participants such as their social status.

In *Culture and Communication*, published in 1976, Leach takes a specifically structural approach, arguing that culture can be interpreted in the same way as language: '*All* the various non-verbal dimensions of culture ... are organised in patterned sets so as to incorporate coded information in a manner analogous to the sounds and words and sentences of a natural language.'[5]

This reference to patterned sets involves another concept central to structuralism, its emphasis on relational meaning: structuralists argue that differential relations between elements in a structure, or patterned set in Leach's term, are more important than any relationship between an individual element and an item outside that structure. For example in terms of language it is argued that the meaning of, for example, cat is constituted less by what it refers to and more by virtue of its difference from other sounds such as caught, cot and sat. Such differential relations, rather than the intentions of the people involved, are regarded as the key to understanding other aspects of culture such as kinship systems and the exchange of goods. It is argued similarly that literary criticism should focus on the structure of the text and not on the intentions of the author or on the relation of the characters to an external reality.

One type of differential relation that is regarded as particularly significant is that of binary oppositions. Saussurean linguistics as developed by Jakobson stresses oppositions that operate on a phonemic level, that is on the level of speech sounds that distinguish between words with different meanings, for example the sounds that distinguish pet from bet. On the level of speech this opposition is regarded as being neutralised in the sound of words such as speak and spend. Structural anthropologists argue that creation and resolution of such oppositions is a fundamental activity of the mind. On the level of culture, they therefore argue that myths, for example, both express an awareness of oppositions and either resolve them or generate further related myths, the most frequently cited opposition being that between nature and culture identified in other oppositions such as those between naked and clothed and raw and cooked.

Leach suggests a similarity between this concept of resolving oppositions and van Gennep's tripartite analysis of rites of passage, which he regards as applying to most types of ritual: 'Most ritual occasions are concerned with movement across social boundaries from one social status to another, living man to dead ancestor, maiden to wife, sick and contaminated to healthy and clean, etc.'[6] He suggests that van Gennep's stages of separation and incorporation represent a form of opposition, between say A and B, while the liminal stage of transition represents a resolution of that opposition being neither A nor B. He also compares the liminal stage to the mediation provided by religion between this world and the divine, a mediation which he refers to as the 'elision of opposites'.[7]

The influence of structuralism is less apparent in Leach's *Social Anthropology*, published in 1982. In this book he argues that 'the various kinds of performance which have, in the past, been assigned to the categories "magic", "religion", "magico-religious" are expressions of artistic creativity rather than misguided attempts to control the material world by mechanical means'.[8] Such performances represent the positive side of magic, while taboos – prohibitions applied to actions, objects and places – are often referred to as its negative side. Leach suggests that such taboos indicate an anxiety about whatever is felt to be abnormal, in terms of being either impure or sacred, both conditions being equally abnormal in relation to ordinary life. In addition, he argues that 'breach of such prohibitions constitutes the prototype of moral evil; the essence of sin is disobedience to a taboo'.[9]

Leach also discusses the difficulties of applying the English categories of magic, religion and ritual to societies that do not have such terms, expressing particular doubt about the usefulness of magic:

> As for magic which readers of Frazer's *The Golden Bough* might suppose to lie at the very centre of the anthropologist's interests, after a lifetime's career as a professional anthropologist, I have almost reached the conclusion that the word has no meaning whatsoever.[10]

Lévi-Strauss

Claude Lévi-Strauss's work emphasises the structuring activity of the mind, and the way this structuring activity imposes pattern on the world by classifying the natural and social environments. As he puts it in an article published in 1949:

> If, as we believe to be the case, the unconscious activity of the mind consists in imposing forms upon content, and if these forms are fundamentally the same for all minds – ancient and modern, primitive and civilised – it is necessary and sufficient to grasp the unconscious structure underlying each institution and each custom, in order to obtain a principle of interpretation valid for other institutions.[11]

He regards it as the anthropologist's task 'to apprehend this unconscious structure'.[12]

This interest in unconscious structure results in a distinction between two types of social behaviour. In a lecture delivered in 1952 Lévi-Strauss expressed this distinction in terms of the 'lived-in orders'[13] and the 'thought-of orders',[14] the latter being those that are unconsciously structured. For Lévi-Strauss the thought-of orders include social structure, described as a model or conceptual representation we construct in order to understand the lived-in order of social relations. Thus he argued that 'the term "social structure" has nothing to do with empirical reality but with models which are built up after it'[15] while 'social relations consist of the raw materials out of which the models making up the social structure are built'.[16]

The thought-of orders consist of symbolic structures. As Lévi-Strauss puts it in an article published in 1950: 'Any culture can be considered as a combination of symbolic systems headed by language, the matrimonial rules, the economic relations, art, science and religion.'[17] These symbolic systems are related: 'All the systems seek to express certain aspects of physical reality and social reality, and even more to express the links that those two types of reality have with each other and those that occur among the symbolic systems themselves.'[18] And their prime concern is communication, with the mind 'reducing to their nature as a symbolic system things which never fall outside that system except to fall straight into incommunicability'.[19]

The distinction between thought-of and lived-in orders is stated in different terms in one of Lévi-Strauss's best known books, *The Savage Mind*, published in 1962, in which he uses instead the Marxist terms superstructure and infrastructure, broadly a society's institutions, ideas and beliefs on the hand and its socio-economic base on the other. It is in superstructure that Lévi-Strauss is interested and which he regards as the province of anthropology: 'It is to this theory of superstructures, scarcely touched on by Marx, that I hope to make a contribution. The development of the study of infrastructures proper is a task which must be left to history.'[20]

In this book Lévi-Strauss develops a contrast between two modes of thought reminiscent of that proposed by Lévy-Bruhl. However, while Lévy-Bruhl distinguished between primitive mentality and Western logic, Lévi-Strauss distinguishes between savage and domesticated thought. In one sense there is a similarity between the two, both being concerned with classification; in another sense there is contrast, savage thought being concerned with the concrete and trying to solve problems as an end in itself, and domesticated thought being concerned with the abstract and trying to solve problems as a means to an end. Lévi-Strauss discusses savage thought primarily in terms of myth, magic and totemic classification; in contrast he describes domesticated thought as primarily historical and scientific.

In discussing myths, Lévi-Strauss argues that savage thought is a particular way of considering and overcoming fundamental logical problems, such as the previously mentioned opposition between nature and culture. Myths can therefore be regarded as a code drawn from the world to elaborate a message not directly about the world. As Lévi-Strauss puts it, it is incorrect 'to think that natural phenomena are what myths seek to explain, when they are rather the medium through which myths try to explain facts which are themselves not of a natural but a logical order'.[21]

While Lévi-Strauss regards magic as characteristic of savage thought and science as characteristic of domesticated thought, he suggests that there are some similarities between the two: 'It is ... better, instead of contrasting magic and science, to compare them as two parallel modes of acquiring knowledge.'[22] This comparison between magic and science aligns Lévi-Strauss with Mauss's argument that both are classificatory systems, in contrast to Durkheim's argument that it is religion and science that constitute such a pair. While Lévi-Strauss's opinion of magic is much more positive than that of the early intellectualists, the comparison also recalls such negative assessments of magic as Frazer's description of it as the bastard sister of science.

Using a very different vocabulary, Lévi-Strauss offers definitions of magic and religion that also resemble those of the intellectualists, although he argues that rather than magic preceding religion the two co-exist. He suggests that religion involves anthropomorphising or personifying natural forces, that is giving nature human shape. Magic, on the other hand, involves what he refers to as the physiomorphism of man, that is giving people the shape of nature, or in other words treating human actions as a part of nature. As he puts it:

> Although it can, in a sense, be said that religion consists in a *humanisation of natural laws* and magic in a *naturalisation of human actions* – the treatment of certain human actions *as if* they were an integral part of physical determinism – these are not alternatives or stages in an evolution. The anthropomorphism of nature (of which religion consists) and the physiomorphism of man (by which we have defined magic) constitute two components which are always given, and vary only in proportion.[23]

Lévi-Strauss relates magic to the fertility rituals practised in totemism – the worship of animals and plants associated with particular social groups. His analysis of these groups shows totemism to have a complex kinship system, raising doubts about both Durkheim's assumption that such groups constitute an elementary social structure and the early intellectualists' assumption that they constitute an early stage in social evolution. In addition, Lévi-Strauss argues that totemism is a complex classificatory system 'based on a postulation of homology [correspondence] between two parallel series – that of natural species and that of social groups'.[24]

Lévi-Strauss contrasts totemic fertility rituals with sacrifice, arguing that the fertility rituals have an objective basis in the natural and social series of totemism, while sacrifice 'makes a non-existent term, divinity, intervene'.[25] In addition, he suggests that the series of natural species used in sacrifice 'plays the part of an intermediary between two polar terms, the sacrificer and the deity, between which there is initially no homology nor even any sort of relation'.[26] As he sums up the difference between totemic rituals and sacrifice: 'One works out a scheme of interpretation while the other sets up (or claims to set up) a technique for obtaining certain results.'[27] Similarly, and returning to structuralism's analogy between culture and language, he adds:

> Classificatory systems belong to the levels of language: they are codes which, however well or badly made, aim always to make sense. The system of sacrifice, on the other hand, represents a private discourse wanting in good sense for all that it may frequently be pronounced.[28]

Godelier and structural Marxism

Lévi-Strauss's structuralism has been accused of ignoring the infrastructure and appearing to isolate the classificatory systems of the superstructure from socio-economic concerns. The work of Maurice Godelier places more emphasis on socio-economic factors and in doing so offers a synthesis between structural and Marxist anthropology.

Godelier's socio-economic emphasis places much of his work outside the scope of this book. However, in an article published in 1973, he discusses the nature of religion, arguing, like Marx, that it is an ideology, a false set of beliefs and ideas which distorts perception of reality. Godelier begins this article by accepting the intellectualist description of religion as explanatory: 'Religion presents itself (as science was to later) as a means and way of knowing reality and explaining it, i.e., accounting for the cause and effect which constitute the order of things.'[29] However, unlike the intellectualists and like Lévi-Strauss, he argues that religion and magic co-exist. As he puts it, because religion represents explanatory causes in a human shape it 'immediately presents itself as a means of action for influencing these ideal characters'.[30] Consequently, 'any religious representation of the world is inseparable from some form of (imaginary) practice, such as prayer, sacrifice, magic, ritual'.[31]

Godelier develops this distinction between religion and magic in terms that recall van Gennep's relation of the former to theory and of the latter to technique:

> As against a certain school of anthropology, which arbitrarily claims a difference in essence between magic and religion, it should be restated that religion exists spontaneously in a theoretical form (representation – explanation of the world) and in a practical form (magic and ritual – influence over the real).[32]

Similarly, and emphasising what he regards as religion's illusory nature, he comments: 'Religion and magic are logically and practically inseparable: they constitute the fundamental and complementary forms for an explanation (illusory) and the transformation (imaginary) of the world.'[33]

Notes

1. Leach 1970: 15.
2. Leach 1970: 16.
3. Leach 1970: 12–13.
4. Leach 1970: 12–13.
5. Leach 1976: 10.
6. Leach 1976: 77.
7. Leach 1976: 72.
8. Leach 1982: 109.
9. Leach 1982: 115.
10. Leach 1982: 133.
11. Lévi-Strauss 1968a: 21.
12. Lévi-Strauss 1968a: 21.
13. Lévi-Strauss 1968b: 313.
14. Lévi-Strauss 1968b: 313.
15. Lévi-Strauss 1968b: 279.

16. Lévi-Strauss 1968b: 279.
17. Lévi-Strauss 1987: 16.
18. Lévi-Strauss 1987: 16.
19. Lévi-Strauss 1987: 37.
20. Lévi-Strauss 1966: 130.
21. Lévi-Strauss 1966: 95.
22. Lévi-Strauss 1966: 13.
23. Lévi-Strauss 1966: 221.
24. Lévi-Strauss 1966: 224.
25. Lévi-Strauss 1966: 228.
26. Lévi-Strauss 1966: 225.
27. Lévi-Strauss 1966: 228.
28. Lévi-Strauss 1966: 228.
29. Godelier 1977a: 178.
30. Godelier 1977a: 179.
31. Godelier 1977a: 179.
32. Godelier 1977a: 179.
33. Godelier 1977a: 182.

9
.
Cognitive approaches
.

I N THE 1970S DECONSTRUCTION replaced structuralism as the
dominant philosophical movement in France. Deconstruction is
primarily a technique for analysing literature that results in multiple
readings of a text: it identifies inconsistencies within a text in such a
way as to create a reading at odds with what the text seems to be
saying, in effect creating a new text that can also be shown to have
inconsistencies, thus creating another reading and another new text
and so on. This emphasis on multiple readings is in marked contrast
to structuralism's search for an ultimate structure. While deconstruc-
tionists accused structuralists of offering too narrow an account of
meaning by reducing it to an invariable structure, some psychologists
regarded structuralism's emphasis on the structuring activity of the
mind as offering too narrow an account of cognition, the subject of
this chapter. Cognition is a broad term referring to how sets of beliefs
are formed and items of knowledge acquired, how they are organised
in the mind, and how they are subsequently used. These mental processes are studied within cognitive science, again a broad term and
involving a range of disciplines, including linguistics, cognitive psychology and artificial intelligence.

One particular type of linguistics is most favoured in cognitive
science, namely what is referred to as generative linguistics. This type
of linguistics emphasises a distinction between deep structure and surface structure similar to that proposed between *langue* and *parole* in
Saussurean linguistics. However, while Saussurean linguistics focuses
on the question of meaning, arguing that a word's meaning resides in
its relation to other words, generative linguistics focuses on the relationship between certain linguistic rules which are said to operate on

the innate and universal level of deep structure, and whose exact nature and extent continue to be debated, and the sentences that are generated on the surface level by those rules.

Saussurean linguistics also has some similarities to one of the other disciplines involved in cognitive science, cognitive psychology. While Saussurean linguistics argues that language mediates our perception of reality, that is acts as an intermediary between us and reality in such a way as to alter our perception of reality rather than simply reflecting it, cognitive psychology analyses a wider range of mental processes which it regards as mediating between the information we receive and our responses to that information. The exact nature of these processes again continues to be the subject of debate. However, many cognitive scientists argue that the mind has various specialised mechanisms, similar to that concerned with language but influencing other cognitive domains, including ones concerned with religion.

Discussion of these cognitive processes has been influenced by recent developments in artificial intelligence – the attempt to create computers capable of performing such tasks as solving problems and understanding languages. It has also been argued that success in such attempts casts light on the processes of human cognition. This in turn involves philosophy in cognitive science because the question of the relationship between machine and human intelligence remains uncertain.

This wide range of ideas about cognition has been applied in various ways to the study of religious beliefs and behaviour and the following discussion presents some examples of those applications, concentrating on the work of four scholars: Sperber, Lawson, McCauley and Boyer.

Sperber
·

In *Rethinking Symbolism*, published in 1974, Dan Sperber's broad argument is that symbolism is less a question of hidden meanings and more a cognitive mechanism that is concerned with irregular types of information. He suggests that there are three cognitive mechanisms, one symbolic and the other two perceptual and conceptual. As he puts it, the symbolic mechanism 'is an autonomous mechanism that, alongside the perceptual and conceptual mechanisms, participates in the construction of knowledge, and in the functioning of the memory'.[1] While this symbolic mechanism is concerned with much more than religion, it can be viewed as helping to explain some of religion's properties.

Sperber also distinguishes between two types of knowledge, symbolic and encyclopedic, a contrast reminiscent of that made by other anthropologists between two modes of thought. Encyclopedic knowledge, that is knowledge about the world, is concerned with trying to avoid contradictions, while symbolic knowledge is constructed from more irregular input: 'The conceptual representations that have failed to be regularly constructed and evaluated constitute the input to the symbolic mechanism.'[2] Sperber suggests similarly that 'all humans learn to treat symbolically information that defies direct conceptual treatment'.[3] In addition, he argues that inconsistencies between encyclopedic and symbolic knowledge can be easily accommodated, citing as an example the Ethiopian Druze who guard their animals from leopards on fast days even though they regard leopards as Christian animals.

Sperber also discusses various earlier interpretations of magico-religious symbolism. He regards the intellectualist analysis of the symbolism in sympathetic magic as being too dismissive, arguing that it fails to recognise that symbolism flourishes in Western societies. He also suggests that approaches that try to identify hidden meanings in symbols are themselves part of the symbolic mechanism: 'All keys to symbolism are part of symbolism itself.'[4] This aligns him with Lévi-Strauss's position that social structure, rather than being symbolised in religion, is itself symbolic. However, Sperber regards Lévi-Strauss's approach as serving to organise symbolic data rather than to interpret it. He also argues against Lévi-Strauss that symbolic systems and language are more different than they are alike: 'Lévi-Strauss has demonstrated the opposite of what he asserts, and myths do not constitute a language.'[5]

Lawson and McCauley

E. Thomas Lawson and Robert N. McCauley relate three cognitive mechanisms to religion, or more specifically to religious ritual, in *Rethinking Religion*, published in 1990 (and summarised in an article by Lawson published in 1993). They begin by proposing a definition of religion which resembles that of the early intellectualists in that it involves a belief in spiritual beings but differs by not restricting ritual to propitiation: 'We construe a religious system as a symbolic-cultural system of ritual acts accompanied by an extensive and largely shared conceptual scheme that includes culturally postulated superhuman agents.'[6]

98

They define ritual acts as consisting of 'a set of actions (including speech acts) of a relatively standard form which manipulate entities (and situations) in the world entertained within the conceptual system'.[7] Specifically religious as distinct from secular ritual involves a religious conceptual system. In addition, they regard religious ritual as instrumental: 'Religious rituals always do something to some thing or somebody. Religious rituals have an instrumental dimension *as construed within the religion's conceptual scheme.*'[8]

Their view of how three cognitive mechanisms combine to produce religious ritual derives from generative linguistics, with the rituals being regarded as operating on the level of surface structure and being generated by the deep structures of the cognitive mechanisms. The first of these cognitive mechanisms is an action-representation scheme containing the sequences of ritual and connecting such abstract elements or slots as agent, action and object. The second cognitive mechanism, a conceptual scheme providing semantic information, specifies the nature of the ritual action. In the case of religious ritual they argue that this information is provided by a religious conceptual scheme that specifies that the slots be filled with religious values, for example that the agent slot be filled with a value such as priest. They regard the third cognitive mechanism, a set of universal and constraining religious principles, the most important of which is the involvement of superhuman agents, as being activated by the application of this religious conceptual scheme to the action-representation scheme.

Boyer

In an article published in 1993 on the cognitive aspects of religious symbolism, Pascal Boyer follows Lawson and McCauley's definition of religion, describing religion as 'the ideas, beliefs, actions and interaction patterns which concern extra-human entities and processes'.[9] However, he defines symbolism in terms similar to those used by Sperber: 'The main idea behind the label "symbolism" is simply that we are dealing with processes and representations that are different from, and more problematic than, what is usually described in everyday domains of knowledge.'[10] As such, symbolism is not restricted to religion: 'It seems more reasonable ... to conceive "symbolism" as non-domain specific, that is, as involving cognitive mechanisms that can be found in everyday thinking too, although perhaps in different configurations.'[11]

Among the theories Boyer discusses in this article is the notion of scripts, in some ways similar to Lawson and McCauley's action-representation scheme for ritual but based instead on research in artificial intelligence:

> The script specifies the actions involved and their order, as well as certain causal relations between them. It is a generic representation, as opposed to a specific memory of a given event sequence, because it specifies conceptual slots that can be filled with particular values.[12]

A further characteristic of scripts is that they can be nested, that is some slots can be filled by sub-scripts. Boyer suggests that religious and everyday scripts can be distinguished in various ways, for example in terms of content and on the level of sub-scripts. In relation to content he comments: 'While everyday scripts are concerned with human actions and the various causal links between them, religious scripts include actions directed at supernatural entities.'[13] On the level of sub-scripts, he argues that everyday sub-scripts have sub-goals while religious sub-scripts are necessary elements in the overall goal.

In *The Naturalness of Religious Ideas*, published in 1994, Boyer relates the widespread recurrence of certain religious ideas and practices to the constraining nature of various cognitive mechanisms: 'Important aspects of religious representations are constrained by universal properties of the human mind-brain.'[14] He suggests that these constraining cognitive mechanisms explain why different religions have so many features in common, such as similarly structured ritual, beliefs in supernatural agencies and in causal connections between such agencies and events, and similar conceptualisations of religious social categories like priest and shaman.

In this book Boyer again relates religion to Sperber's interpretation of symbolism, arguing that supernatural events and agencies are intuitively perceived to be unnatural, or as irregularly constructed in Sperber's terms. As Boyer puts it: 'People have some cognitive means, of which they are not necessarily aware, of sorting out events and states that violate intuitive expectations from events and states that do not.'[15] What remains uncertain is the basis on which this sorting out proceeds, or as other anthropologists have expressed it, what throws the switch from one, sacred code, to another, secular code.

Notes

1. Sperber 1975: xii.
2. Sperber 1975: 141.
3. Sperber 1975: 148.
4. Sperber 1975: 50.
5. Sperber 1975: 83.
6. Lawson and McCauley 1990: 5.
7. Lawson and McCauley 1990: 5.
8. Lawson and McCauley 1990: 125.
9. Boyer 1993a: 4.
10. Boyer 1993a: 24.
11. Boyer 1993a: 25.
12. Boyer 1993a: 22.
13. Boyer 1993a: 39.
14. Boyer 1994: viii.
15. Boyer 1994: 36.

10

·

Feminist approaches

·

P ROVIDING AN EXACT DEFINITION of feminism is difficult because of the range of thought it contains. Identifying exactly when it began presents similar problems. However, one aspect of feminism is a concern with equal rights for women and an end to discrimination against them. Corresponding to the period covered by this book, *A Vindication of the Rights of Woman* is often cited as an early example of such rights-oriented feminism. This work, written by the British author Mary Wollstonecraft (1759–97) and published in 1792, was influenced by the principles of the French Revolution and applied the emerging concern with political rights to the social, educational and domestic position of women. Marxist analysis of perceived social inequities has also influenced some more radical forms of feminism.

Another often cited influence on the development of feminism was the Industrial Revolution, also regarded as having contributed to the establishment of sociology as an academic discipline. The term, originating in an analogy with the French Revolution, refers to the industrial transformations of the past two to three centuries, which have affected both how things are made, using industrial processes rather than traditional forms of manufacture, and where people live, in urban rather than rural areas. Another development associated with these industrial transformations is the inclusion, particularly in periods of war, of increasing numbers of women in the work force.

One of the equal rights for which women campaigned was the right to vote, achieved in the first half of the twentieth century at different times in different places: Australia, in 1902, was one of the first countries to give women the vote; the Soviet Republic followed in 1917, Britain in 1918, initially restricting the right to women over 30, and the United States in 1920; France, in 1944, was one of the last European countries to extend the vote to women. The search for women's equality with men continues in other areas. For example, in relation to religion it is argued that women priests should be allowed in Catholicism. And in relation to the study of religion it has been pointed out that anthropology, despite being literally the study of man in the sense of human, is often led in Britain by men in the sense of male:

> Despite the prominence of women in Malinowski's seminars, none became head of a department of anthropology. This is perhaps less surprising when one notes how rare it was until very recently for women to be appointed heads of departments in any subject in universities, but the position outside Britain was different.[1]

It has also been argued that such social inequalities are linked to an androcentric, that is male-centred, bias in scholarship which has resulted in, for example, sources relating to women being ignored, sources relating to men being interpreted as if representative of both sexes, and sources relating to both sexes being interpreted only from the perspective of men. This argument has been advanced in particular in relation to the study of literature, with feminist scholars reviving books written by women and reappraising ones written by men. However, it has also been advanced in the study of religion, for example in a recent analysis of women's involvement in religions of the Greco-Roman world: *Her Share of the Blessings*, written by Ross Shepard Kraemer, an American professor of religious studies, and published in 1992.

Kraemer begins this book by arguing that, until the past two decades, women's involvement in religion has largely been ignored, a lack of interest which she attributes to 'the insidious, significant, and unarticulated assumption that human religion and human history were identical with men's religion and men's history'.[2] Kraemer also suggests that traditional scholarship has distorted the study of Judaism and Christianity in the Greco-Roman period by screening the sources, for example ignoring non-literary sources such as private correspondence and burial inscriptions, which tend to be more informative about women; misrepresenting other sources, for example presenting biased translations of literary texts; and making untested assumptions, for example assuming that anonymous authors were men.

In her analysis of women's involvement in Greco-Roman religions,

Kraemer relies partly on the grid/group model developed by the anthropologist Douglas, which relates different types of religion to different types or sections of society defined in terms of grid and group as two dimensions of social experience. In doing so, Kraemer argues that until fairly recently developments in the study of religion within the social sciences have been given short shrift in humanities disciplines: 'Ironically, although feminist scholars have amply demonstrated the pitfalls of androcentric approaches when it comes to describing women's religious experiences and activities, many bring similar enough theological agendas to share the biases of their male colleagues against social science approaches.'[3]

Other feminist scholars have discussed religion more generally as contributing to social inequalities, in turn raising the question of how such inequalities should be remedied, for example through a sex-neutrality that goes beyond the polarities of a culture regarded as androcentric or through a sex-differentiation that reinterprets the polarities. The following discussion concentrates on the work of two such scholars, one from the United States and the other from Continental Europe.

Kristeva

The French scholar Julia Kristeva belongs to the broad movement referred to as post-modernism whose philosophical positions have included structuralism and deconstruction. However, in her work in both linguistics and psychoanalysis Kristeva has maintained an independent perspective. For example, in an article published in 1973 she argues that structuralism is only capable of apprehending 'the field of practices which do no more than subserve the principle of social cohesions, of the social contract'.[4] In her view it cannot apprehend such practices as art, ritual and certain aspects of myths, that is 'practices which, although they do subserve social communications, are at the same time the privileged areas where this is put to non-utilitarian use, the areas of transgression and pleasure'.[5] Similarly she suggests that structuralism 'has no way of apprehending anything in language which belongs not with the social contract but with play, pleasure or desire'.[6]

While Kristeva's linguistic interests have led her to query structuralism, her work as a psychoanalyst has contributed to her doubts about deconstruction, discussed in an article published in 1982. Here she contrasts deconstruction's emphasis on infinite text-related meanings with the need to achieve a truth in psychoanalysis that cures the patient and in doing so relates to external reality. While this truth is not constant, being constructed in the specifics of a psychoanalytic session, it can be judged in terms of its effect. As Kristeva puts it: 'This analytic interpretation is only, in the best of cases, *partially true*, and its truth, even though it operates with the past, is demonstrable only by its *effects in the present*.'[7]

Kristeva's more specifically feminist work includes an article published in 1979 which discusses the development of feminism, and an analysis of the implications of the Judaeo-Christian religious tradition which was published in 1974 as part of a longer work. It is on these two publications that the following discussion concentrates.

Kristeva begins her discussion of the development of feminism by distinguishing between three concepts of time. One is the linear time of history which she regards as masculine. The other two are repetition and eternity, or, as Kristeva also refers to them, cyclical time, 'the eternal recurrence of a biological rhythm which conforms to that of nature',[8] and monumental time which is almost outside concepts of temporality. She relates monumental time to myths of resurrection, arguing that such myths 'perpetuate the vestige of an anterior or concomitant maternal cult, right up to its most recent elaboration, Christianity, in which the body of the Virgin Mother does not die but moves from one spatiality to another ... via assumption'.[9] While cyclical and monumental time are linked to female consciousness, motherhood and reproduction, Kristeva adds that they are 'the fundamental, if not the sole, conceptions of time in numerous civilizations and experiences'.[10]

Kristeva argues that the earlier rights-oriented generation of feminists sought equality with men, or in other words 'aspired to gain a place in linear time'.[11] In contrast, the second generation, emerging after 1968, emphasised a radical difference between men and women and situated itself outside linear time and within cyclical or monumental time. She suggests that the first generation faced the problem of loss of identity in conforming to linear time while the second runs the risk of becoming a kind of inverted version of what it opposes. She identifies a third generation of feminists, currently forming, whose task is to encompass these three concepts of time while moving in the direction of a consciousness that allows individual difference and is no longer dependent on specific sexual identity.

The question of anterior maternal cults is also discussed in Kristeva's analysis of the Judaeo-Christian religious tradition in which she argues that 'long before the establishment of the people of Israel, the

Northern Semites worshipped maternal divinities'.[12] She relates the development of Judaism to the displacement of these female deities by the principle of a male, paternal divinity, suggesting that within this development 'monotheism represses, along with paganism, the greater part of agrarian civilizations and their ideologies, women and mothers'.[13] As part of this process of repression women were excluded from power and knowledge, and sexual differences were emphasised: 'No other civilization seems to have made the principle of sexual difference so crystal clear: between the two sexes a cleavage or abyss opened up.'[14]

Kristeva argues that Western societies have retained this repressive monotheistic ideology, for example in 'transmission of the name of the father',[15] with Christianity adding its own particular emphasis. She suggests that, while Christianity is less exclusive of women than Judaism, it demands a price for their inclusion: to be included women must abandon 'the orgasmic maternal body'[16] and keep their virginity, represented by the Virgin Mary and her impregnation through the paternal word or Holy Spirit. Kristeva adds that such abandoning of the mother, and of what the mother represents, is not restricted to Christianity, citing the Greek myth in which Electra, the daughter of Clytemnestra and Agamemnon, persuades her brother to avenge their father by killing his murderess Clytemnestra and her lover.

Daly

Two books by the American feminist theologian and philosopher Mary Daly are discussed in this section, one in which she advocates a sex-neutral approach to resolving inequalities and the other in which she favours a sex-differentiated approach. In both books Daly regards established religion as an aspect of patriarchy, literally the rule of the father and indicating a view that men oppress women by exercising institutional and ideological control over them.

Daly's *Beyond God the Father*, published in 1973, is both a condemnation of traditional religion and in a way an attempt to create a new one. Her condemnation of religion is primarily directed against Christianity and Judaism, which she regards as supporting the oppression of women:

> The symbol of the Father God, spawned in the human imagination and sustained as plausible by patriarchy, has in turn rendered service to this

type of society by making its mechanisms for the oppression of women appear right and fitting. If God in 'his' heaven is a father ruling 'his' people, then it is in the 'nature' of things and according to divine plan and the order of the universe that society be male-dominated.[17]

However, she thinks that other religions are similarly culpable, arguing that 'the symbolic and linguistic instruments for communication – which include essentially the whole theological tradition in world religions – have been formulated by males under the conditions of patriarchy'.[18] Consequently it is 'inherent in these symbolic and linguistic structures that they serve the purposes of patriarchal social arrangements'.[19]

Among the instances of patriarchy that Daly discusses are the theodicies that religion generates. She argues that attempts to relate human success and suffering to divine favour and disfavour are also used to justify social inequalities. As she puts it: 'As marginal beings who are coming into awareness, women are in a situation to see that "God's plan" is often a front for men's plans.'[20] Daly argues similarly that the Biblical myths of Eve's creation from Adam's rib and of her role in tempting Adam to sin, what Christians refer to as the Fall, have created a negative image of women and justified their oppression. However, she indicates that such myths can be taken from their patriarchal context and given a positive interpretation:

One could see the myth as prophetic of the real Fall that was yet on its way, dimly glimpsed. In that dreaded event, women reach for knowledge and, finding it, share it with men, so that together we can leave the delusory paradise of false consciousness and alienation.[21]

As this quote suggests, Daly's aim is not only to analyse what she regards as religion's contribution to the oppression of women but, in doing so, to create a new religion by liberating women from patriarchy: 'The becoming of women implies universal human becoming. It has everything to do with the search for ultimate meaning and reality, which some would call God.'[22] As part of this search she suggests a change in the conception of God, from a masculine noun to a sex-neutral verb of being. Transforming women's consciousness is part of the process of transforming the concept of the divine: 'The unfolding of God, then, is an event in which women participate as we participate in our own revolution.'[23]

Daly also refers to Eliade's argument that Western societies have lost touch with the sacred in a psychically damaging way. She suggests that, if so, this is little loss because sacred symbols and myths have perpetuated oppression. Instead a new consciousness can 'bring us away not only from the false paradise of the pseudo-sacred symbols of patriarchy but also from the banal nonreligious consciousness that Eliade deplores'.[24] In doing so 'it can bring us into a new meeting with the sacred'.[25]

This new consciousness is not restricted to women, with Daly suggesting that what both sexes should seek is a type of sex-neutral wholeness or androgyny. This term, from the Greek for male (*andro*) and female (*gyno*), indicates that, rather than performing their traditional, socially conditioned roles, men should develop feminine qualities and women masculine qualities, dissolving the differences, and thus the inequalities, between the sexes. As Daly puts it: 'The healing process demands a reaching out toward completeness of human being in the members of both sexes – that is, movement toward androgynous being.'[26]

Androgyny is abandoned in Daly's *Gyn/Ecology*, published in 1978, being replaced, as the book's title suggests, by gynocentric separation. While the divine continues to be described as a process of being, use of the word God is also abandoned, being replaced by Goddess. However, in this book Daly places more emphasis on a type of inner spirituality similar to that associated with the New Age Movement and discussed in the following chapter. Thus, for example, the Goddess is described as 'the divine spark of be-ing in women'.[27] Daly's use of hyphenation in this quote indicates a further feature of this book: language is modified to produce new meanings. Some of these meanings are directed against men, such as stag-nation and mal(e)-functioning, while others give a positive value to terms often applied negatively to women. For example, Daly relates spinster to spinning, one of her central images describing women's participation in the process of becoming: 'Spinsters spinning out the Self's own integrity can break the spell of the fathers' clocks.'[28]

The reference in the book's title to ecology indicates Daly's wider range of concerns, discussing various practices in addition to Christianity that she regards as patriarchal and destructive of both the environment and women: 'As Gyn/Ecologists, we feel a deep communion with our natural environment. We share the same agony from phallocratic attack and pollution as our sister the earth. We tremble with her.'[29] As before, her aim is to expose these patriarchal practices, in doing so encouraging women to leave patriarchy behind and create a new identity for themselves. Among the practices she discusses are the Hindu ritual in which a woman burns herself to death on her husband's funeral pyre, Chinese foot-binding, African circumcision of women, American gynaecology and European witch-burning.

Daly's approach to the last of these, the burning of alleged witches by Christians in the fifteenth, sixteenth and seventeenth centuries, has two main elements: one is an analysis of the events, the other is an analysis of how modern historians have discussed them. While it is not possible to calculate how many women were murdered in this period as a result of witchcraft beliefs, discussed under the category of magic by many of the scholars referred to in earlier chapters, Daly suggests that 200,000 is a conservative estimate. She relates the murder of these women to various factors. For example, describing how the women were accused of sexual misbehaviour, she suggests that this reflects a tendency among men to project their own sexual fantasies on to women. She also argues that most of the victims were spinsters and widows who were not assimilated into patriarchy and were targeted for that reason. In addition, she suggests that many were midwives and healers opposed by the male medical profession.

Daly's analysis of how modern, male-authored scholarship has discussed these events concludes that in addition to dying in history, these women have mainly died from history: 'It is the custom of historians of the early modern period to omit discussion of the witch-craze. Usually the omission is almost, but not quite, absolute.'[30] Daly regards most of the exceptions to this process of historical erasure as being flawed. One such instance she discusses is a scholar who takes a functional approach, regarding the parts of a society as contributing to the functioning of the whole, and suggests that certain witch trials may have been a means of establishing what types of behaviour were socially acceptable and a therapeutic way of resolving social conflicts. As Daly concludes: 'Although he does not state *for whom* it was therapeutic, we may safely assume that it was not so for the murdered women.'[31]

Notes

1. Kuper 1996: 119–20.
2. Kraemer 1993: 4.
3. Kraemer 1993: 12.
4. Kristeva 1986a: 26.
5. Kristeva 1986a: 26.
6. Kristeva 1986a: 26.
7. Kristeva 1986d: 309.

8. Kristeva 1986c: 191.
9. Kristeva 1986c: 191.
10. Kristeva 1986c: 192.
11. Kristeva 1986c: 193.
12. Kristeva 1986b: 140.
13. Kristeva 1986b: 141.
14. Kristeva 1986b: 141.
15. Kristeva 1986b: 151.
16. Kristeva 1986b: 147.
17. Daly 1985: 13.
18. Daly 1985: 22.
19. Daly 1985: 22.
20. Daly 1985: 30.
21. Daly 1985: 67.
22. Daly 1985: 6.
23. Daly 1985: 40.
24. Daly 1985: 68.
25. Daly 1985: 68.
26. Daly 1985: 50.
27. Daly 1984: 183.
28. Daly 1984: 387.
29. Daly 1984: 409.
30. Daly 1984: 206.
31. Daly 1984: 209.

Afterword

.

Secularisation
assessed

MANY OF THE SCHOLARS discussed in the preceding chapters
have argued that religion is in decline, a process referred to as
progressive secularisation. For example, Marx thought the coming of
communism would bring religion to an end, while the intellectualists
discussed cultural evolution as beginning with magic, moving on to
religion and culminating in science. In proposing such developments,
these scholars regarded them as beneficial, that is as doing away with
a form of delusion. Other scholars, such as Jung and Eliade, identified a similar process of secularisation but regarded it as harmful, that
is as representing a form of spiritual decline. It is the accuracy of
these reports of religion's decline that this book ends by discussing.

One of the problems in assessing secularisation is that the term has
various meanings. In a narrow sense secularisation can be viewed as
a process of separating religion from other institutions. It thus
involves, for example, an end to state support for religion, to legisla-
tion that reflects religious beliefs, and to censorship that safeguards
religion. However, more broadly secularisation involves a decline in
religious beliefs and practices. This aspect of secularisation is discussed by Jeffrey K. Hadden in an article published in 1987 in which
he examines opinion polls conducted in the United States between
approximately 1945 and 1985. He argues that these polls fail to support the theory of progressive secularisation: 'When one examines the
large corpus of literature that provides some longitudinal perspective,
I don't see how one can fail to conclude that religion stubbornly
resists the prophecies of its early demise.'[1]

Among the figures Hadden cites are that the proportion of Americans reporting a belief in God fluctuated little during the period cov-

ered and never fell below 94 per cent. Similarly in 1985 almost as many people reported that they prayed as did in 1948 (87 per cent in 1985 and 90 per cent in 1948). The figures relating to church membership, at about 70 per cent, and attendance, at about 40 per cent, were also stable. However, within this broad picture of stability in American religious beliefs and practices, he suggests that various changes occurred. For example, he argues that liberal, Protestant church traditions, that is the American religious mainstream, lost membership and influence while evangelical and fundamentalist traditions experienced sustained growth.

As further evidence contradicting the theory of progressive secularisation Hadden points to religion's continuing political influence around the world, for example in the conflicts between Catholics and Protestants in Northern Ireland and between Israelis and Arabs in the Middle East. He argues that the assumption that religion's influence has declined has hindered analysis of such conflicts: 'Because of our assumptions about secularization, we have systematically engaged in a massive wholesale dismissal of the religious factor when considering socio-political events in the modern world.'[2] Hadden also points to other examples of religious involvement in the political, such as the Muslim overthrow of the Shah of Iran in 1979 and the role of liberation theology, a Christian theology that understands God as demanding social justice, in promoting socialism in South America and elsewhere. As Hadden puts it: 'The extensiveness of political entanglement around the globe is simply too great to be ignored.'[3]

Such political involvement indicates the continuing influence of traditional religions. In addition, the formation of new religious configurations also contradicts the theory of progressive secularisation, as Hadden points out in discussing the countercultural religious movements that have arisen in the United States since the 1960s and have involved a search for an alternative to Western values. As he puts it: 'The search for a "new consciousness" took many bizarre turns, but there was a profound religious quality to the search for new meaning.'[4]

Such new religious movements form part of the discussion in Paul Heelas's *The New Age Movement*, published in 1996. Focusing on developments in Britain and the United States, Heelas describes the New Age Movement as a spectrum of cultural behaviour ranging from the world-rejecting at one end to the world-affirming at the other and united by a sense of the inner self as sacred, 'an *internalized* form of religiosity'.[5] According to Heelas, New Agers are committed to a search for this inner spirituality, regarded as more authentic than the self created by social conditioning, and often by extension to a search for the spirituality of the natural order as a whole.

Heelas associates the movement with the middle to upper-middle professional classes in particular. He describes the world-rejecting wing of the New Age as dating from the late 1960s and including such countercultural developments as hippies and their rejection of what are regarded as the capitalistic externals of life. He dates the world-affirming or prosperity wing of the New Age to slightly later, arguing that it regards inner spirituality as a means to an external end and relating it to the teaching and training provided by, for example, Scientology and seminar organisations such as est (Erhard Seminars Training) and Transformational Technologies.

Heelas suggests that New Agers regard inner spirituality as providing a kind of magical power, contradicting Weber's thesis of religion becoming less magical and this-worldly. As Heelas puts it:

> To varying degrees and in various ways, New Agers typically maintain that 'magical' energy (as it might be termed, in anthropological fashion) is available to make a difference. For some, the difference concerns what 'actually' takes place in the 'external' world; for others, the difference has to do with what takes place in experience. Whatever the case, the fact remains that New Agers generally insist that they are able to call upon inner spirituality to improve their health, their prosperity, their relationships, and so on.[6]

Heelas argues that, as part of its opposition to established authorities, the New Age rejects the external authority of religious institutions. However, he suggests that New Agers regard all religions as sharing an 'inner, esoteric core'[7] and that they therefore select from different religious traditions what is relevant to their search for inner spirituality, favouring, for example, the Zen school of Buddhism and the Vedantist school of Hinduism. The objection to authority and perception of an inner continuity between religions also enable New Agers to draw from other religious traditions, both from the present, such as Native American religions, and the past, such as Gnosticism, ancient Egyptian religion, and Celtic and Druidic religions, as well as from such modern developments as Jung's concept of individuation, a psychotherapeutic process intended to foster self-fulfilment.

Heelas's broad thesis is that the New Age Movement is a response to certain aspects of the modern world, such as uncertainties about personal identity, which is itself framed by other aspects of the modern world, such as a sense of self that is detraditionalised or individualistic as distinct from sociocentric or collectivistic. As he puts it:

'Various uncertainties of modernity generate identity problems which propel people to do something about their situation; various certainties of modernity direct such people to seek solutions by way of New Age provisions.'[8]

While establishing the extent of the New Age Movement is difficult, various opinion polls provide some indicators. For example, Heelas cites an opinion poll carried out in Britain in 1993 which indicated that 40 per cent of the population believed in some form of spirit or life-force. An earlier poll, conducted in 1989, indicated that 72 per cent of the population identified a sacred presence in nature. Opinion polls carried out in the 1970s in the United States estimated that some six million Americans had been involved in transcendental meditation (4 per cent of the population), five million in Yoga, nine million in spiritual healing and ten million in Eastern mysticism. In relation more to the prosperity wing of the movement, Heelas estimates 'that *at least* five million people have taken the seminars of the est-like organizations since the early 1970s'.[9] Heelas also points to a growth of interest in Britain in Eastern spirituality, citing a claim that 'Buddhism is the fastest growing religion in Britain at the present time'.[10] In addition, he suggests that interest among younger people is increasing in paganism, a broad term encompassing both shamanism and witchcraft. Establishing the number of pagans is again difficult but Heelas refers to a study of paganism in the United States which 'puts the figure at around 300,000'.[11]

Like Hadden, Heelas also points out that some forms of traditional religion continue to flourish: 'Traditions, established and regulated forms of life, have not disappeared. Fundamentalistic Christianity, perhaps attracting some 60 million in the USA, shows no signs of withering away.'[12] To end by returning to one of the scholars discussed earlier, the evidence analysed by Heelas and Hadden contradicts the theory of progressive secularisation and indicates both the survival of established religions and the formation of new religious configurations, thus supporting Durkheim's conclusion that 'there is something eternal in religion which is destined to survive all the particular symbols in which religious thought has successively enveloped itself'.[13]

Notes

1. Hadden 1997: 353.
2. Hadden 1997: 358.

3. Hadden 1997: 358.
4. Hadden 1997: 355.
5. Heelas 1996: 29.
6. Heelas 1996: 25–6.
7. Heelas 1996: 28.
8. Heelas 1996: 137.
9. Heelas 1996: 111–12.
10. Heelas 1996: 55.
11. Heelas 1996: 132.
12. Heelas 1996: 144.
13. Durkheim 1976: 427.

Bibliography

.

T HE REFERENCES IN THIS bibliography are to the most recent, or most readily available, editions in English of the publications cited in the text. Three further publications, to each of which this book is indebted, can be recommended to readers interested in longer accounts of developments in the study of the sacred: E. E. Evans-Pritchard's *Theories of Primitive Religion* (Oxford: Oxford University Press) which was published in 1965 and is therefore now slightly dated but has the twin advantages of being both concisely and immaculately written, and two books whose titles reflect the particular interests of their authors, John Macquarrie's *Twentieth-century Religious Thought: The Frontiers of Philosophy and Theology, 1900–1980* (London: SCM Press), published in a revised edition in 1981 which was reprinted in 1983, and Brian Morris's *Anthropological Studies of Religion* (Cambridge: Cambridge University Press), published in 1987 and last reprinted in 1996.

Beattie, J. H. M. (1970), 'On understanding ritual', in Wilson 1970, p. 240ff.

Boyer, Pascal (1993a), 'Cognitive aspects of religious symbolism', in Boyer 1993b, p. 4ff.

Boyer, Pascal (ed.) (1993b), *Cognitive Aspects of Religious Symbolism*, Cambridge: Cambridge University Press.

Boyer, Pascal (1994), *The Naturalness of Religious Ideas*, Berkeley: University of California Press.

Daly, Mary (1984), *Gyn/Ecology: The Metaethics of Radical Feminism*, London: The Women's Press.

Daly, Mary (1985), *Beyond God the Father: Toward a Philosophy of Women's Liberation*, Boston: Beacon Press.

Douglas, Mary (1970), *Purity and Danger*, Harmondsworth: Pelican Books.

Douglas, Mary (1973), *Natural Symbols*, Harmondsworth: Pelican Books.

Douglas, Mary (1975a), 'Pollution', in Douglas 1975b, p. 47ff.

Douglas, Mary (1975b), *Implicit Meanings*, London: Routledge & Kegan Paul.

Durkheim, Émile (1976), *The Elementary Forms of the Religious Life*, London: George Allen & Unwin.

Eliade, Mircea (1959), *The Sacred and the Profane*, New York: Harcourt, Brace & World.

Eliade, Mircea (1979), *Patterns in Comparative Religion*, London: Sheed and Ward.

Engels, Friedrich (1957a), '*Anti-Dühring* (Extracts)', in Marx and Engels 1957, p. 144ff.

Engels, Friedrich (1957b), 'Ludwig Feuerbach and the end of classical German philosophy', in Marx and Engels 1957, p. 214ff.

Engels, Friedrich (1957c), 'Engels to C. Schmidt', in Marx and Engels 1957, p. 276ff.

Evans-Pritchard, E. E. (1937), *Witchcraft, Oracles and Magic among the Azande*, Oxford: Oxford University Press.

Evans-Pritchard, E. E. (1956), *Nuer Religion*, Oxford: Oxford University Press.

Frazer, J. G. (1990), *The Golden Bough*, London: Macmillan.

Freud, Sigmund (1985a), *Totem and Taboo*, in Freud 1985b, p. 49ff.

Freud, Sigmund (1985b), *The Pelican Freud Library 13*, Harmondsworth: Pelican Books.

Geertz, Clifford (1993a), 'Ritual and social change', in Geertz 1993c, p. 142ff.

Geertz, Clifford (1993b), 'Religion as a cultural system', in Geertz 1993c, p. 87ff.

Geertz, Clifford (1993c), *The Interpretation of Cultures*, London: Fontana Press.

Giddens, Anthony (ed.) (1997), *Sociology: Introductory Readings*, Cambridge: Polity Press.

Godelier, Maurice (1977a), 'Fetishism, religion and Marx's general theories concerning ideology', in Godelier 1977b, p. 169ff.

Godelier, Maurice (1977b), *Perspectives in Marxist Anthropology*, Cambridge: Cambridge University Press.

Goody, Jack (1961), 'Religion and ritual: a definition problem', *British Journal of Sociology* 12, p. 142ff.

Hadden, Jeffrey K. (1997), 'Challenging secularization theory', in Giddens 1997, p. 351ff.

Heelas, Paul (1996), *The New Age Movement*, Oxford: Blackwell Publishers.

Hegel, G. W. F. (1984), *Lectures on the Philosophy of Religion 1: The Concept of Religion*, Berkeley: University of California Press.

Hegel, G. W. F. (1985), *Lectures on the Philosophy of Religion 3: The Consummate Religion*, Berkeley: University of California Press.

Hegel, G. W. F. (1987), *Lectures on the Philosophy of Religion 2: Determinate Religion*, Berkeley: University of California Press.

Horton, Robin (1970), 'African traditional thought and western science', in Wilson 1970, p. 131ff.

Horton, Robin (1973), 'Lévy-Bruhl, Durkheim and the scientific revolution', in Horton and Finnegan 1973, p. 249ff.

Horton, Robin and Ruth Finnegan (eds) (1973), *Modes of Thought*, London: Faber & Faber.

Jarvie, I. C. (1964), *The Revolution in Anthropology*, London: Routledge & Kegan Paul.

Jarvie, I. C. (1984), *Rationality and Relativism*, London: Routledge & Kegan Paul.

Jarvie, I. C. and Joseph Agassi (1970), 'The problem of the rationality of magic', in Wilson 1970, p. 172ff.

Jung, Carl (1958a), 'Psychology and religion', in Jung 1958b, p. 3ff.

Jung, Carl (1958b), *The Collected Works of C. G. Jung 11*, London: Routledge & Kegan Paul.

Jung, Carl (1968a), 'Archetypes of the collective unconscious', in Jung 1968c, p. 3ff.

Jung, Carl (1968b), 'The concept of the collective unconscious', in Jung 1968c, p. 42ff.

Jung, Carl (1968c), *The Collected Works of C. G. Jung 9/1*, London: Routledge & Kegan Paul.

Jung, Carl (1970a), 'Archaic man', in Jung 1970b, p. 50ff.

Jung, Carl (1970b), *The Collected Works of C. G. Jung 10*, London: Routledge & Kegan Paul.

Kraemer, Ross Shepard (1993), *Her Share of the Blessings*, Oxford: Oxford University Press.

Kristeva, Julia (1986a), 'The system and the speaking subject', in Moi 1986, p. 24ff.

Kristeva, Julia (1986b), 'About Chinese women', in Moi 1986, p. 138ff.

Kristeva, Julia (1986c), 'Women's time', in Moi 1986, p. 187ff.

Kristeva, Julia (1986d), 'Psychoanalysis and the polis', in Moi 1986, p. 301ff.

Kuper, Adam (1996), *Anthropology and Anthropologists*, London: Routledge & Kegan Paul.

Lawson, E. Thomas (1993), 'Cognitive categories, cultural forms and ritual structures', in Boyer 1993b, p. 188ff.

Lawson, E. Thomas and Robert N. McCauley (1990), *Rethinking Religion: Connecting Cognition and Culture*, Cambridge: Cambridge University Press.

Leach, Edmund (1970), *Political Systems of Highland Burma*, London: The Athlone Press.

Leach, Edmund (1976), *Culture and Communication*, Cambridge: Cambridge University Press.

Leach, Edmund (1982), *Social Anthropology*, Oxford: Oxford University Press.

Lessa, William A. and Evon Z. Vogt (eds) (1965), *Reader in Comparative Religion*, New York: Harper & Row.

Lévi-Strauss, Claude (1966), *The Savage Mind*, London: Weidenfeld and Nicolson.

Lévi-Strauss, Claude (1968a), 'Introduction: history and anthropology', in Lévi-Strauss 1968c, p. 1ff.

Lévi-Strauss, Claude (1968b), 'Social structure', in Lévi-Strauss 1968c, p. 277ff.

Lévi-Strauss, Claude (1968c), *Structural Anthropology*, London: Allen Lane The Penguin Press.

Lévi-Strauss, Claude (1987), *Introduction to the Work of Marcel Mauss*, London: Routledge & Kegan Paul.

Lévy-Bruhl, Lucien (1926), *How Natives Think*, London: George Allen & Unwin.

Malinowski, Bronislaw (1982a), 'Magic, science and religion', in Malinowski 1982b, p. 17ff.

Malinowski, Bronislaw (1982b), *Magic, Science and Religion and Other Essays*, London: Souvenir Press.

Marett, R. R. (1914a), 'Pre-animistic religion', in Marett 1914d, p. 1ff.

Marett, R. R. (1914b), 'From spell to prayer', in Marett 1914d, p. 29ff.

Marett, R. R. (1914c), 'Introduction', in Marett 1914d, p. xxiff.

Marett, R. R. (1914d), *The Threshold of Religion*, London: Methuen.

Marx, Karl (1957), 'Contribution to the critique of Hegel's philosophy of right', in Marx and Engels 1957, p. 41ff.

Marx, Karl and Friedrich Engels (1957), *Marx and Engels: On Religion*, Moscow: Foreign Languages Publishing House.

Marx, Karl and Friedrich Engels (1965), *The German Ideology*, London: Lawrence and Wishart.

Mauss, Marcel (1972, written in collaboration with Henri Hubert), *A General Theory of Magic*, London: Routledge & Kegan Paul.

Moi, Toril (ed.) (1986), *The Kristeva Reader*, Oxford: Basil Blackwell.

Otto, Rudolf (1950), *The Idea of the Holy*, Oxford: Oxford University Press.

Radcliffe-Brown, A. R. (1956a), 'Taboo', in Radcliffe-Brown 1956c, p. 133ff.

Radcliffe-Brown, A. R. (1956b), 'Religion and society', in Radcliffe-Brown 1956c, p. 153ff.

Radcliffe-Brown, A. R. (1956c), *Structure and Function in Primitive Society*, London: Cohen & West.

Skorupski, John (1976), *Symbol and Theory: A Philosophical Study of Theories of Religion in Social Anthropology*, Cambridge: Cambridge University Press.

Smart, Ninian (1997), *Dimensions of the Sacred: An Anatomy of the World's Beliefs*, London: Fontana Press.

Smith, Jonathan Z. (1978a), 'Good news is no news: aretalogy and gospel', in Smith 1978b, p. 190ff.

Smith, Jonathan Z. (1978b), *Map is not Territory*, Leiden: E. J. Brill.

Spencer, Herbert (1885), *A System of Synthetic Philosophy 6: Principles of Sociology 1*, London: Williams and Norgate.

Sperber, Dan (1975), *Rethinking Symbolism*, Cambridge: Cambridge University Press.

Tambiah, S. J. (1985a), 'The magical power of words', in Tambiah 1985c, p. 17ff.

Tambiah, S. J. (1985b), 'Form and meaning of magical acts', in Tambiah 1985c, p. 60ff.

Tambiah, S. J. (1985c), *Culture, Thought and Social Action: An Anthropological Perspective*, Cambridge, MA: Harvard University Press.

Tambiah, S. J. (1990), *Magic, Science, Religion and the Scope of Rationality*, Cambridge: Cambridge University Press.

Titiev, Mischa (1965), 'A fresh approach to the problem of magic and religion', in Lessa and Vogt 1965, p. 316ff.

Turner, Victor (1957), *Schism and Continuity in an African Society*, Manchester: Manchester University Press.

Turner, Victor (1967a), 'Symbols in Ndembu ritual', in Turner 1967d, p. 19ff.

Turner, Victor (1967b), 'Colour classification in Ndembu ritual', in Turner 1967d, p. 59ff.

Turner, Victor (1967c), 'Betwixt and between: the liminal period in *rites de passage*', in Turner 1967d, p. 93ff.

Turner, Victor (1967d), *The Forest of Symbols*, Ithaca: Cornell University Press.

Turner, Victor (1968), *The Drums of Affliction*, Oxford: Oxford University Press.

Turner, Victor (1969), *The Ritual Process*, London: Routledge & Kegan Paul.

Tylor, E. B. (1929a), *Primitive Culture 1*, London: John Murray.

Tylor, E. B. (1929b), *Primitive Culture 2*, London: John Murray.

van Gennep, Arnold (1960), *The Rites of Passage*, London: Routledge & Kegan Paul.

Weber, Max (1978), *Economy and Society*, Berkeley: University of California Press.

Weber, Max (1991a), 'The social psychology of the world religions', in Weber 1991b, p. 267ff.

Weber, Max (1991b), *From Max Weber: Essays in Sociology*, London: Routledge.

Wilson, Bryan R. (ed.) (1970), *Rationality*, Oxford: Basil Blackwell.

Index

.